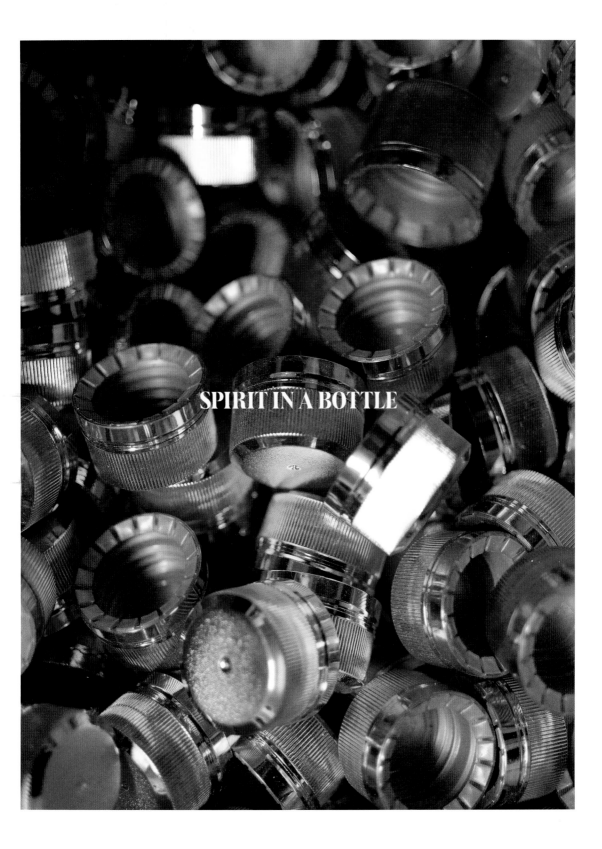

SPIRIT IN A BOTTLE

SPIRIT IN A BOTTLE

TALES & DRINKS FROM TITO'S HANDMADE VODKA

Tito's

Handmade

VODKA

AUSTIN ★ TEXAS

HARVEST
An Imprint of WILLIAM MORROW

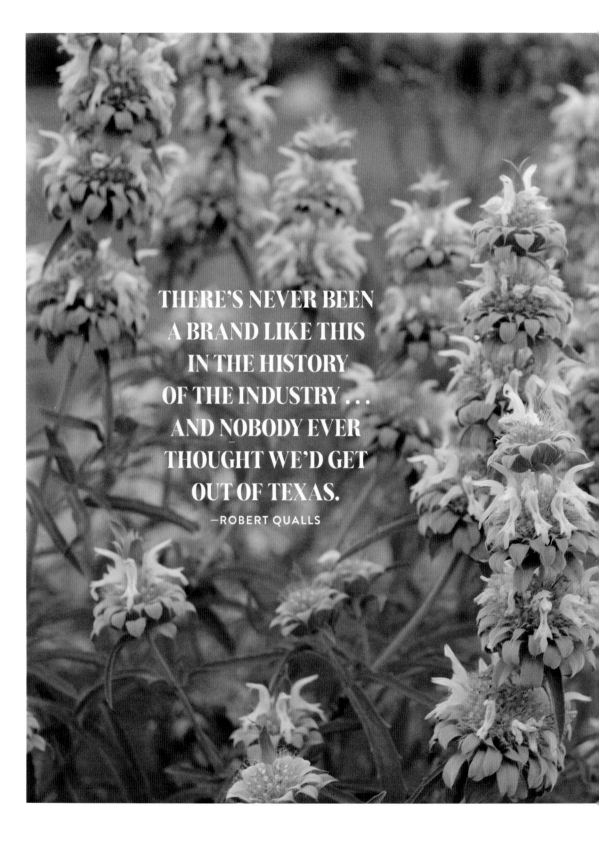

THERE'S NEVER BEEN
A BRAND LIKE THIS
IN THE HISTORY
OF THE INDUSTRY . . .
AND NOBODY EVER
THOUGHT WE'D GET
OUT OF TEXAS.

—ROBERT QUALLS

Robert believed in Tito's Handmade Vodka way
back in the beginning. A veteran in the industry,
he was one of our first distributors and, many years
later, became part of the Tito's team.

Robert was the kind of genuine, loyal friend who
anybody would be lucky to meet in their lifetime.
Smart, optimistic, and perpetually beaming,
Robert was a true gentleman with a heart bigger
than the state he was born in. He saw something
special and took a chance on Tito's when no one
else would. Safe to say we wouldn't be here
today without him.

Here's to Robert and everyone else who believed
in Tito's Handmade Vodka along the way.

In memoriam
ROBERT QUALLS
1957–2021

CONTENTS

FOREWORD

Tito's Handmade Vodka, the First Legal Distillery in Texas!" This was the headline that first caught my eye, piquing my interest that morning in early 1999 as I sat at my desk at the Bellagio, casually perusing a trade magazine. I read on and discovered that Tito's was currently available in six states and, lucky for me, Nevada was one of them. I tracked down the distributor and gave my friend a call at DeLuca (now Breakthru Beverage Group) to ask if I could get a sample.

"You can have as much as you want," he replied. "We can't give the stuff away!"

I said to myself: "Self?"

"Yes, Tony?"

"What's missing with this brand is education and awareness."

The next day, two bottles of Tito's sat on my desk, and upon tasting it I thought, "This is good, this is different." So I quickly blind-tasted the brand with several of our bartenders, and they all had the same reaction. We decided that Tito's would make a great addition to our vodka selection at the Bellagio, and since we were focused on education and product knowledge, we would also invite Tito to come and present his vodka to our 150-plus bartenders and bar apprentices along with more than 200 waitstaff.

The next day I looked up the phone number for Mockingbird Distillery and called; a gentleman answered immediately.

"I'm looking for a Mr. Tito Beveridge."

"This is Tito," the gentleman replied.

I introduced myself as the Bellagio's Property Mixologist and Cocktail Developer, and explained how I had just tried his vodka, loved it, and planned to bring it into the resort's twenty-nine bars and restaurants, but first I'd like him to come visit us in Las Vegas, teach our staff about his vodka, and tell his story. The phone was silent for a few moments and then came his reply.

"I can't do that, sorry."

Now, at this point I was a little dumbfounded, as no one had ever before said no to being invited to the Bellagio to present their products. Little did I know that Tito himself was doing everything at that time—distilling the juice (in a homemade still), filtering, diluting, bottling, labeling, looking for distribution, and basically trying to get people to sample his vodka. Coming to Las Vegas would mean shutting down production for several days—and, I didn't know it then, but he was basically flat broke. So I thanked Tito for his time, gave him my contact information should he change his mind, and wished him the best of luck with his vodka.

About a week or so later, my associate Andrea said there was a Tito Beveridge on the phone for me.

"Hi, Tito, how are you?"

"When would you like me to come?"

The story Tito tells is that his wife stopped by the distillery (referred to as the Shack), saw my name and the Bellagio on a piece of paper tacked to the bulletin board, and asked him what it was all about. When Tito told her about our call, she convinced him to go. In fact, I'm not sure she gave him a choice.

Tito came and spoke in front of more than three hundred Bellagio staff over the course of three days, and as you can imagine, the team fell in love with his vodka, but they also fell in love with Tito and his story. In the days that followed, when a guest ordered vodka, the reply would likely be "Have you ever tried

Tito's? It's distilled down in Austin, Texas (from the first legal distillery in the state), and is corn-based, gluten-free, and the smoothest vodka you'll ever sip."

There were very few "micro" or "craft" distilleries in the United States then, and to my knowledge, those that existed were not making and marketing vodka. Jörg Rupf founded St. George Spirits in 1982 as an eau de vie distillery in Emeryville, California, at a time when there were very few distilleries in the United States. In 1983, Miles Karakasevic started producing brandy in Ukiah, California, changed the name to Domaine Charbay in 1991, and introduced fruit-flavored vodkas in 1998. Anchor Distilling began in 1993 by Fritz Maytag; his Junipero Gin became the first craft gin post-Prohibition. But when Tito's launched in 1997, it was really the first American premium craft vodka to hit the market.

Fast-forward twenty-five years. I went to visit Tito, and he hasn't changed much since those early days. He picked me up in his old SUV, and we promptly ran out of gas on the way to his ranch. We went swimming, and when I got stung by a wasp, Tito rubbed window cleaner on it; sure enough, the sting and swelling went away. We ate Texas BBQ at an outside joint, drank beer, went to a rodeo, and he gave me a cowboy hat. And we visited the distillery, which has expanded beyond the Shack. But even though the production has grown—a lot—the care that goes into each bottle is the same as it was when he first made it. I had met him at a time when he was doing everything by hand; today the same philosophy applies, just on a much larger scale.

At the time this book went to press, there were more than 190 legal distilleries in Texas, putting the state in the top five producers in the country. Thank you very much, Mr. Beveridge, for leading the way!

Happiness!
TONY ABOU-GANIM
The Modern Mixologist

BREAKING LAS VEGAS

It may have been a gamble, but Tony took a chance on Tito's even when the odds were against us.

Here's to that fateful trip to Vegas, and to Tony for believing in our dream way back then.

———— ★ ————

Unlike dry vermouth, white vermouth is much sweeter, with notes that balance the herbal qualities in Yellow Chartreuse. The combination softens the sweetness found in both liqueurs and elevates the cocktail's citrus and spice.

1½ ounces Tito's Handmade Vodka
1 ounce Dolin Blanc Vermouth de Chambéry
½ ounce Yellow Chartreuse
2 dashes of orange bitters
1 lemon peel, for garnish

Add the Tito's, white vermouth, Yellow Chartreuse, and orange bitters to a mixing glass with ice. Stir and strain into a chilled martini glass. Garnish with the lemon peel.

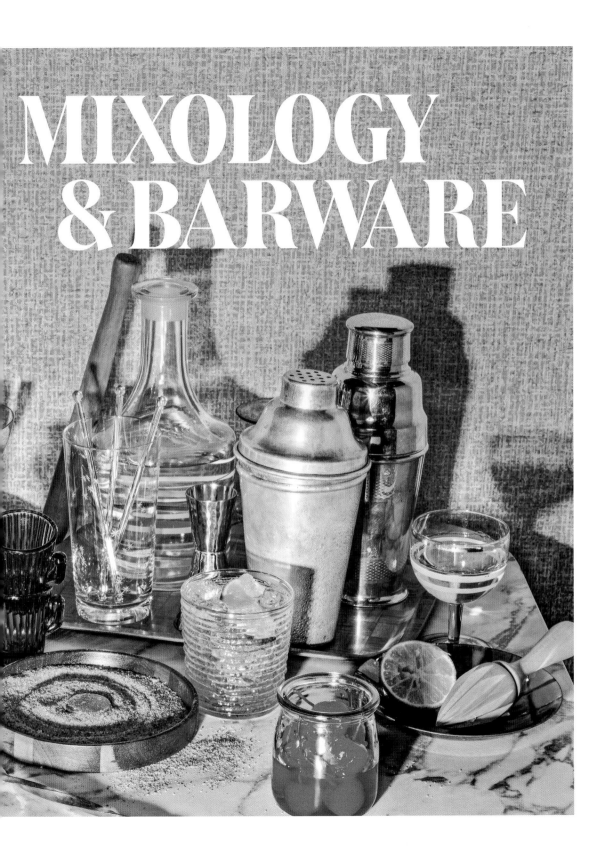

MIXOLOGY & BARWARE

MIXOLOGY

Modern mixology has been around since the mid-1800s, evolving over centuries to eventually bring you your favorite cocktail. (With any luck, that cocktail's somewhere in this book.)

While flavor trends, garnish techniques, glassware, and even the popularity of infusions have changed with the times, the foundation of mixology has remained tried and true: As long as you've got the right spirit (and you've got the right spirit), you're equipped to practice the art of mixology. Consider it a spectrum. For some, it's a well-loved, highly skilled artistry that requires the meticulous craft of a pastry chef. For others, it's making sure the punch tastes good for the party.

Whether you're happy with the skills you have or are striving for top-tier tricks of the trade, our goal is to lend a hand along the way.

And remember, when in doubt, experimentation is at the heart of it all. Have a good time, taste-test often, and call every practice run your own personal cocktail hour.

To start, let's cover the most important piece of the mixology puzzle: balance.

Cocktails range from sweet to bitter, tart to spicy, light and crisp to heavy and dynamic, but each one, no matter the profile, has to strike a balance.

For example, take the Tito's Mule (page 41)—simultaneously sweet, spiced, crisp, and tart. It's simple, made with only three ingredients, but creates balance within its flavor profile. The spice of the ginger is mellowed with smooth Tito's, and the sweetness of both is cut slightly with fresh citrus. There's harmony to every sip.

Achieving balance is both an art and a science; precision and feeling. Avoid overwhelming your cocktail with one specific flavor or element (e.g., a gimlet that sips a little too sweet or a bloody that just tastes like soup). The hard part in creating balance is choosing the right ingredients and learning the best way to combine them. The easy part is tasting as you go until you've got that perfect sip.

Once you've locked in your key ingredients, consider:

TEMPERATURE

Whether a drink is served up or on the rocks, ice is an unlisted ingredient in every single chilled cocktail. While ice gives your drink its perfect temperature, it also dilutes as it melts— which isn't always a bad thing. Make your ice with high-quality H_2O if you can (it'll be part of your drink one way or another).

EXPERIMENTATION

Following the steps in this book will always lead you to a mean cocktail. However, when inspiration strikes and you want to make a cocktail that tastes like a peanut butter and jelly sandwich, experiment to get the perfect pour. Just like cooking, taste everything and improvise.

PERSONALITY

Don't love one of the ingredients listed in a recipe? Swap it for something else. Eager to see how grapefruit pairs with vanilla but the recipe calls for orange? Go for grapefruit. These recipes are tasty and always a safe bet, but they also act as a foundation for any cocktail builds you can think up.

BARWARE

We aren't too fussy about what you use to shake and sip your cocktails. We love a good substitution, whether it's a lemon for a lime or a screw-top jar for a cocktail shaker. The heart of mixology is figuring out how to do what you want with what you've got.

Tool	Purpose	How to Use	Alternatives
JIGGER	**MEASURING LIQUID:** The most important tool for consistency. We like one with two ends: a 1½-ounce side and a 1-ounce side. When you stick with exact measurements, you can trust your cocktail will turn out delicious every time.	Carefully pour any liquid you need and measure accordingly.	A standard shot glass is 1½ ounces. No shot glass? A measuring cup works just fine (as long as it has ounce measurements).
SHAKER	**SHAKING:** When it comes to shakers, metal shaker tins are the best. Why? Because metal will let you know when your drink has reached the ideal temperature. If you're mixing up a chilled cocktail, the outside of your shaker will get frosty, and when it's ice cold to the touch, you'll know it's time.	Add your ingredients to a shaker, top it off with the lid or pint glass, and give it a shake. When it's time to pour or strain, knock the area where lid meets shaker to release the seal.	Use a jar with a lid. Just keep an eye on your cubes and the temperature of your cocktail.
MIXING GLASS	**THE SPACE TO STIR:** You know how martinis are served either shaken or stirred? This is what you use when you prefer the latter.	Add your ingredients to a mixing glass and stir using a bar spoon or household alternative.	A wide-mouth jar or large glass should do the trick.
SPOON	**STIRRING:** Why a nice, long, twisted bar spoon? When you're stirring your drink, it's going to help you get just the right amount of water off those ice cubes without struggling against your ingredients.	Place the handle of the spoon between your pointer finger, middle finger, and thumb. With a loose hold, stir in a wide circle, twisting as you go.	Skip the soup spoon and use a chopstick.

We do, however, want to share the most useful tools to have on hand when cocktail hour calls. If you know what you do need, it's easier to understand what you don't need, and there are a lot of gizmos and gadgets out there.

Yes, having the right tool does play a part in a delicious cocktail, but there's more than one way to get there . . . and when a recipe says you need a julep strainer for this or a Hawthorne strainer for that, but all you have is a colander, we're here to tell you that's A-OK. Your home bar is just that—yours.

Tool	Purpose	How to Use	Alternatives
MUDDLER	**BREAKING IT DOWN:** When you want to smash some berries, get the juice and pulp out of an orange, or release the oils from some herbs, your muddler is there for you.	Add your ingredients to a shaker, mixing glass, or cocktail glass—based on your recipe—and, using the end of your muddler, mash the ingredients together until they've reached the desired consistency.	Turn a wooden spoon upside down and use the end of the handle.
STRAINER	**FOR A CLEAN POUR:** When your cocktail is shaken up, leave the ice, seeds, leaves, or anything else you wouldn't want to drink behind.	Top your shaker or mixing glass with a strainer and carefully pour the liquid into a new glass.	If you're using a shaker-pint-glass combo, create a small space between shaker and glass and pour carefully. And when in doubt, just use a mesh strainer or cheesecloth.
STIR STICK	**FINISHING TOUCH:** Unlike the bar spoon, the stir stick is reserved for your cocktail glass, to give your drink a final mix before you sip.	Not all cocktails require this, so follow the recipe before you start stirring.	Glass or metal straw, chopstick, or, hell, your finger as long as it's clean and in your drink alone.
COCKTAIL RIMMER	**COAT THE RIM:** From textural contrast to enhancing the flavor of your cocktail, including salt, sugar, spices, or something sweet on your glass's rim will add a dynamic touch to your cocktail experience.	For most recipes, run a citrus slice along the rim of your glass. If your recipe doesn't call for citrus, try simple syrup (page 159) or honey. Then flip your glass upside down into the rimmer and roll the glass's rim in salt, sugar, or whatever your recipe calls for.	A small plate to hold the salt, sugar, or spice works just fine.

ICONS & CLASSICS

If you're trying to figure out your passion, find something you love to do that you're good at.

—TITOISM #1

What I like to do	What I'm Good at
1. Be around people	1. Engineering
2. air conditioning	2. Science
3. build things	3. problem solving
4. Night Life	4. dealing with people
5. Music	5. sales
6. Talk to girls	6. Inventing things
7. Travel	7. Numbers

Draw a line down the middle of a piece of paper.

On one side: list what you're good at.

On the other: list what you like to do.

Now, wrap a job around it.

You might see a dream you've always had. Or maybe you uncover something new. If you're lucky, you might have already found whatever's there, and that paper just proves it's where you need to be.

It was the early '90s, and on a kitchen table sat our founder's résumé: mortgage lending, oil drilling, water testing, roughnecking, a couple degrees. In the background, a staticky television played a late-night infomercial, its host guiding a live audience on how to find their passion and purpose.

Draw a line down the middle of a piece of paper . . .

The result, now sitting on the back of that résumé? A vodka company.

The dream itself might've happened overnight, but bringing it to life would take a few more years. Searching for photos of old moonshiners to learn how to construct a homemade pot still, scrapping together parts to actually build the thing, figuring out a recipe, taste-testing and taste-testing, learning the ins and outs of an unchartered industry, and getting people to try a vodka that came out of a stock bottle with a paper label—those steps were just the beginning.

But we got there. With a lot of grit, a lot of debt, a lot of perseverance, and even more patience.

And that scrawled-out list started it all.

TITO'S NEAT

Make a vodka so smooth you can drink it straight.

—TITOISM #6
BY WAY OF A LIQUOR STORE OWNER IN THE MID-'90S

The ten simple words that guided us to that perfect recipe.

———— ★ ————

Tito's mixes well with just about anything. The way you enjoy a cocktail is up to you, but before you flip through these pages, do us a favor: Pour a finger or two of Tito's into your favorite glass. At room temperature. No garnishes. Just the vodka. Give it a sip and get to know the spirit behind our story.

TITO'S WATER LEMON

Once you've been acquainted properly, feel free to add ice, water, and lemon to your glass. Crushed or cubed, purified or straight from the tap, one good squeeze or a fully submerged slice, that's up to you.

Back in the day, our distillers nixed the ice and lemon and just topped off their water bottles with a splash of Tito's. They called it Sweetwater.

Consider this its elevation.

1½ ounces Tito's Handmade Vodka
4 ounces still water
1 lemon slice

A cocktail so simple you don't even need directions.

TITO'S SODA LIME

Have you ever ordered a Tito's and Vodka? It happens.

Fortunately, most bartenders know what you mean. And will even add lime.

1½ ounces Tito's Handmade Vodka
4 ounces sparkling water
1 or 2 lime slices

Pour the Tito's and sparkling water over ice and squeeze in a lime slice (or two). Yep, it's that easy. So easy you might call it Tito's and Vodka.

★

Our Vodka Is Distilled from Corn, so It's Naturally Gluten-Free

Tito's Handmade Vodka is certified gluten-free by the Gluten-Free Certification Organization. Some folks add a bit of mash back into the spirit after distillation, which could add gluten, but not us.

TITO'S ALL-TIME FAVORITE

Two Tito's employees walk into a bar.

One orders a Tito's Soda Lime. The other, a Tito's Soda Orange. Between the table and the bar, the server forgets who wanted what, so out come two glasses topped with a slice of each.

A spritz here, a squeeze there, and just like that a minor slip-up became an all-time favorite. An icon, even.

1½ ounces Tito's Handmade Vodka
4 ounces sparkling water
1 orange slice
1 lime slice

Add everything to a glass with ice and give it a spin.

TITO'S PLUS ONES AND THEIR PLUS UPS

We all have a go-to. Tito's and a splash of something. The Plus Ones you invite to every party.

But when the next party writes "no jeans" on the invite, dress things up a little and turn that Plus One into a *Plus Up*.

TITO'S & LEMONADE
The Plus One

When life hands y—
    The juice is worth the sq—
    [Insert phrase about zest and life].
    You get it.

———— ★ ————

1½ ounces Tito's Handmade Vodka
4 ounces lemonade
1 lemon slice, for garnish
1 fresh mint sprig, for garnish, optional

Just add the Tito's and lemonade to a glass with ice. Stir and garnish with a lemon slice. Really want to freshen things up? Add a mint sprig too.

The Plus Up
TITO'S GARDEN PARTY

Tito's has always been distilled and bottled in Austin, Texas. You know about the barbecue, country music, big hats, and riding our horses to work,* but you may not know about the blanket of rosemary that creeps across the state. It's in every garden, sprouts up in backyards across cities, and lines neighborhood streets. It may as well grow wild at this point. Needless to say, it's pretty easy to pick a few sprigs and throw 'em in a cocktail.

————— ★ —————

* *We don't actually ride horses to work.*

The thing about rosemary is that it triggers multiple senses; the flavor profile is subtle, but its aroma is strong, offering a dynamic drinking experience. A fresh sprig paired with bright citrus will activate your taste buds before you even take a sip.

1½ ounces Tito's Handmade Vodka
1 ounce fresh lemon juice
¾ ounce simple syrup (page 159)
2 ounces sparkling water
2 lemon slices, for garnish
1 fresh rosemary sprig, for garnish

Add the Tito's, lemon juice, and simple syrup to a shaker with ice. Shake and strain into a glass with fresh ice. Top with the sparkling water and stir. Garnish with the lemon slices and a sprig of rosemary. Better yet, use your sprig as a stir stick for an even stronger flavor.

The Plus Up
TITO'S CHILTON

Not a rosemary fan? Swap it for a salted rim and create the Chilton for an equally refreshing sip.

Salt, to rim your glass
1½ ounces Tito's Handmade Vodka
2 ounces sparkling water
1 ounce fresh lemon juice

Rim your glass with salt (page 5) and fill with ice. Add all ingredients and stir.

TITO'S & ORANGE JUICE
The Plus One

In life, there are mimosa people and there are screwdriver people. We accept all drink proclivities, but it should come as no surprise that we have a preference.

Weekend brunches, holiday mornings, early flights. They all call for a Tito's and OJ.

1½ ounces Tito's Handmade Vodka
4 ounces orange juice
1 orange slice, for garnish

Just add the Tito's and orange juice to a glass with ice. Stir and garnish with an orange slice.

DISCLAIMER: *You don't need to book a flight to give this cocktail a try.*

The Plus Up
TITO'S TAKES FLIGHT

Screwdrivers on an early flight. That's a special kind of unspoken cocktail hour.

Tito's wasn't always on those in-flight menus. But in the early 2000s, when our cases slowly started selling, we had an idea. How do you get thousands of people to try a vodka they've never heard of? Put it in the sky.

It started with cold calling, then blindly emailing folks in the airline industry, then waiting. And waiting. And hearing plenty of "no." Until one day, we got a text from someone who worked for one of the largest airlines in the country. And he really liked Tito's. "There's a spot open for Tito's Handmade Vodka, if you can get us a lot of it in not a lot of time."

We didn't even have a line at the distillery for those small airline-mandated plastic bottles. But with a heavy pour of bootstrapping and a newly installed bottling line, we were on our first flight ninety days later.

So, when you take that next vacation . . . or are actually heading to your in-laws but want to feel like you're on vacation, grab a bottle of coconut water before you board and toast to the members of the Tito's team who gave our copper cap its wings.

Coconut water's hydrating properties make it the perfect choice for stuffy plane cabins (especially if you were out late the night before). The acidity from the citrus is cut by the coconut water's neutrality, creating a well-balanced sip with a tropical twist.

50 mL Tito's Handmade Vodka
(aka mini, nip, mini-bottle, shooter, or whatever your specific region of the world calls it)

3 ounces sparkling water
1 ounce coconut water
¼ ounce orange juice

Add all ingredients to a cup with ice and stir.

TITO'S & CRANBERRY
The Plus One

Order that vodka cran with pride. Especially when that vodka is Tito's.

1½ ounces Tito's Handmade Vodka
4 ounces cranberry cocktail
1 lime slice, for garnish

Just add the Tito's and cranberry cocktail to a glass with ice. Stir and garnish with a lime slice.

The Plus Up
TITO'S COSMO

Cosmos. Tito's.
Frosted tips. Acid wash.
Just like every generation, the '90s had its highs and lows. Fortunately, the decade did us a lot of good—it helps that we share it with a timeless classic.

The sharpness found in the cranberry and lime cuts through the sweetness of the orange liqueur, lightening its syrupy nature. Plus, a well-rounded cocktail should be as pretty to look at as it is to drink.

1½ ounces Tito's Handmade Vodka
1 ounce orange liqueur
¾ ounce cranberry cocktail
½ ounce fresh lime juice
1 lime wheel or lemon twist, for garnish

Add the Tito's, orange liqueur, cranberry cocktail, and lime juice to a shaker with ice. Shake and strain into a martini glass. Garnish with a lime wheel or lemon twist.

TITO'S MARTINI

No vermouth, never any vermouth.

—TITOISM #3

Skipping the vermouth is an unofficial company rule, though we know many martini connoisseurs would disagree.

Either way, a martini lets the spirit shine. Shaken, not stirred, for a colder cocktail. Extra-dry and a twist. Or if you're like some folks at Tito's, three blue-cheese-stuffed olives.

★

3 ounces Tito's Handmade Vodka
3 olives or 1 lemon twist, for garnish

Just add the Tito's to a shaker with ice. Shake or stir (we prefer shaking), and strain into a chilled martini glass.

Prefer it dirty? Add olive juice. Extra-dry? Vermouth rinse. Reverse it, skip it; how you enjoy a martini is up to you.

If you're reading this and your heart is racing at the mere thought of ordering a martini, never mind making one, we've got you covered. It may not seem easy, but we promise, it can be.

Choose Your Own Martini Order

Start with style. A martini can be wet—more vermouth, captures less of the spirit. Or dry—less vermouth, captures more of the spirit. Extra-dry has little to no vermouth. And finally, bone-dry has no vermouth and is our preference. Any martini can be dirty (just add olive juice) or filthy (add more).

Then choose your preferred technique. Shaking a martini breaks down the ice, which dilutes your drink and possibly leaves ice crystals. Stirring cools down your cocktail with less dilution.

Decide how you'd like it served. Straight up is the classic way: no ice, served in a martini glass. On the rocks is a martini over ice (hey, to each their own).

Finally, choose your garnish. An onion is most commonly served with a gin martini. A twist is just a fancy lemon peel; it's classic, but you can try lime, orange, or grapefruit. Olives can be paired with a dirty or non-dirty martini. We prefer them stuffed with blue cheese.

Our Martini Order

Tito's martini, bone-dry (no vermouth, please), shaken, up, blue-cheese-stuffed olives.

But you could keep it simple and just say "Tito's martini, bone-dry, with olives" and, most likely, you'll be delivered something pretty similar.

TITO'S ESPRESSO MARTINI

There are a few "unofficial, official" drinks of the Tito's team. The espresso martini is one of them. It's the cocktail that starts the party, ends it, or for some, does both.

No matter where you go, the Tito's Espresso Martini will look and taste a little different; each bar has its own special recipe, flair, or signature garnish. Who knows, this recipe might end up being your new favorite.

———— ★ ————

A classic espresso is often enjoyed with a spoonful of granulated sugar, which allows the rich, nutty coffee flavor to shine while cutting its overwhelming bitterness. Consider the Tito's Espresso Martini a replica of that process. The sweetness of coffee liqueur complements the bitter espresso, making each sip as smooth as the last. Add a splash of cream, and your cocktail will resemble a latte or cappuccino.

> 2 ounces Tito's Handmade Vodka
> 1 ounce coffee liqueur
> 1 ounce espresso
> ½ ounce simple syrup (page 159)
> ½ ounce creamer, optional
> 3 espresso beans, for garnish

Add the Tito's, coffee liqueur, espresso, simple syrup, and creamer (if using; we prefer it sans creamer) to a shaker with ice. Shake and strain into a martini glass. Garnish with the espresso beans.

TITO'S TRANSFUSION

"What the hell's a Transfusion?"

It's Tito's and grape juice and a few other things. It's surprisingly delicious. Ya know, for having grape juice in it.

It's another one of those "unofficial, official" cocktails, but this time for the green—a putt-putt course, a backyard, or from a seat at the clubhouse bar, any type of green will do.

———— ★ ————

Grape and ginger ale are an underrated pairing; together they brighten each individual flavor while blending into a perfect combination of sweetness and effervescence. Citrus points the spotlight on the two, elevating and creating a quencher for the course.

> 2 ounces Tito's Handmade Vodka
> 2 ounces ginger ale
> 1 ounce Concord grape juice
> ¼ ounce fresh lime juice
> 1 grape, for garnish
> 1 lime slice, for garnish

Add the Tito's, ginger ale, grape juice, and lime juice to a glass with ice and stir. Garnish with a grape and a lime slice.

TITORITA

Occasionally, folks think Tito's is a tequila. Now we're sharing this recipe for a margarita, which doesn't really help the confusion. Let us clarify.

Tito's is a vodka and also happens to taste great in a 'rita. So great, we felt compelled to adjust the name a little: TitoRita. Sure, we've gotten some strange looks ordering one, but we haven't steered you wrong yet.

And when you do order one (c'mon, give it a try), ask for half the orange liqueur. That's how we prefer it.

———— ★ ————

The TitoRita: a perfect example of acidity paired with sweet. On its own, such a large quantity of lime juice would be too overwhelming to sip on, but mixing it with orange liqueur and agave creates balanced viscosity and flavor. Tito's, compared to the tequila used in a traditional margarita, offers a lighter take without creating an entirely new profile. Why add salt to a 'rita? Salt acts as a magnifying glass for the ingredients it's paired with, intensifying the flavors every time you sip from the rim.

Salt, to rim the glass, optional
2 ounces Tito's Handmade Vodka
½ ounce orange liqueur
2 ounces fresh lime juice
¼ ounce agave nectar
1 lime slice, for garnish

If you like a salted rim, coat the edge of your glass with salt (see page 5). Next, add the Tito's, orange liqueur, lime juice, and agave to a shaker with ice. Shake and pour everything into a glass and garnish with the lime slice.

TITO'S BLOODY MARY

The Brunch Hero.

It's a staple across midday menus, a signature pairing to your eggs benny, and, in some cases, something to snack on while you wait for pancakes.

The true beauty of the Bloody is how you can make it your own (especially when you make it at home). No spice or extra spice. Infused with cucumber or black pepper and garlic. Green tomatoes instead of red. And garnishes. So. Many. Garnishes.*

———— ★ ————

*We could list them all, but our publisher says we can't go over word count.

There's something about sipping a Bloody after a long night out. Tomato juice has salt and vitamin C, giving you the boost you need, while the spice wakes up your taste buds. Despite its savory notoriety, there's a slight sweetness that comes from the tomato itself and is immediately balanced with the umami flavors found in Worcestershire. Even if you're a "sweet" breakfast person, starting your Saturday with a Bloody sets the palate up for a successful weekend.

1½ ounces Tito's Handmade Vodka
4 ounces DIY Bloody Mary Mix (recipe follows) or your favorite Bloody Mary mix
Whatever garnish you can think up (see Tito's Tip, page 39)

Just add the Tito's and Bloody Mary mix to a glass with ice. Stir and add your garnishes.

DIY BLOODY MARY MIX

4 ounces tomato juice
1 to 3 dashes of Worcestershire sauce
2 to 4 dashes of hot sauce
Horseradish, to taste
A squeeze of fresh lime juice
Fresh cracked black pepper

Combine all the ingredients in a glass and stir.

BATCH BLOODY MARY MIX

16 ounces tomato juice
4 to 6 dashes of Worcestershire sauce
6 to 8 dashes of hot sauce
Horseradish, to taste
¼ cup of fresh lime juice
5 to 7 cracks of fresh cracked black pepper

Add all the ingredients to a resealable container. Refrigerate for up to 3 days.

Tito's Tip

Go wild with your garnishes. Try celery stalks, olives, dill pickles, pickled green beans, lemon slices, parsley sprigs, bacon, cheese cubes, boiled shrimp, crab legs, an entire mini-cheeseburger on a skewer. The world is your Tito's Bloody Mary.

Look for the Copper Cap

Our signature way of standing out on shelves, backbars, and bar carts: When you're looking for Tito's, just find the copper cap.

TITO'S MULE

We'll call it a coincidence that a mule is traditionally served in a copper mug and that we distill Tito's using copper in our stills, and that a Tito's Mule served in a Tito's Copper Mug is a cocktail as classic as they come.

Back in the mid-'90s, we started distilling in makeshift stills, rigging together spare parts, junkyard finds, and salvaged copper.

These days, we don't frequent the junkyard, but we do use copper in our pot stills to make our vodka. And everything from our copper mugs to our copper cap is an ode to those early days and to the still that got us started.

Ginger and citrus: sweet, spicy, and sour. The fun part is determining how you want the balance to play out. Ginger beers have different levels of spice, some tasting like you just took a bite from the root itself. When in doubt about which to choose, just know that the lime will round out the cocktail to your perfect level of drinkability.

   1½ ounces Tito's Handmade Vodka
   3 ounces ginger beer
   ½ ounce fresh lime juice
   1 lime slice, for garnish

Add the Tito's, ginger beer, and lime juice to a Tito's Copper Mug with ice. Stir, and garnish with the lime slice.

WHAT IS A POT STILL, ANYWAY?

In short, a pot still is a vessel that conducts heat to distill alcohol. Like a tea kettle, but for vodka.

Our first still was a 16-gallon rig, heated up on a turkey fryer (we're serious), some metal tubing as a condenser, and the receiving tank from an old Dr Pepper barrel. It was made entirely from salvaged parts and used direct fire, which occasionally resulted in hot vodka spraying absolutely everywhere, but it made booze, so we kept going.

These days, we've refined the system and craft the spirit using old-fashioned pot stills, taste-testing every batch. Our process, similar to that used to make fine single-malt scotches and high-end French Cognacs, requires more skill and effort, but we think it's well worth it.

That copper shimmer you see on our label is a symbol of the pot still that helps make Tito's, *Tito's*.

The Shack in Austin, Texas (see page 70)

The original still room, early 2000s

INFUSED & CRAFTED

Next time you walk into your local liquor store, take a look at the bottles lining the shelves. Once you get past the classics, what do you see? Blue raspberry, sour cherry, orange vanilla, coconut tropical breeze. Flavors of all varieties. Vodka that tastes like candy or fruit; vodka that smells a little like sunscreen or cinnamon gum. See what we're getting at?

Back before we knew Tito's would be Tito's, we tried our hand at infusions. Jars full of fresh berries or hot peppers topped with bottom-shelf vodka. They were a hit, given as homemade gifts or requested by friends who wanted a flavored vodka made exactly how they liked it.

But liquor stores didn't need more of what they already had—vodkas that tasted like something else. No; what they needed was a vodka so smooth you could sip it straight: a vodka-flavored vodka.

We took note and set out to do one thing and do it right. But you can give infusing a try for yourself. Start with our spirit, and then make it your own: sweet or savory; fruity or spicy. After some time, you'll get the perfect bottle that tastes exactly how you want it, and you'll know exactly what's in it.

Think of Tito's as a blank canvas (that happens to taste pretty good on its own). Whatever your personal touch might be, we guarantee it's something you can't find on a shelf.

Plus, those do-it-yourself infusions still make great gifts. The vodka's just gotten better.

HABANERO INFUSION & FIRESTARTER

Did you know that habanero peppers infuse really quickly? Neither did we.

Habanero was our first go at this . . . and maybe a risky prototype to discover the ins and outs of homemade infusions. We grabbed a handful, sliced 'em up, added vodka, and walked away for a week.

Then we let people try it.

Like we said, risky. But that's the beauty of trial-and-error. Eventually you figure it out, even if figuring it out means a mouthful of fire. Now we use two peppers at most and let it sit for about 30 minutes. Then, just for safe measure, we stick it in the freezer. This way you taste the pepper, feel the heat, and cool it down all in one sip.

HABANERO INFUSION

1 or 2 habanero peppers
750 mL Tito's Handmade Vodka

Slice the habaneros and remove the seeds. We suggest wearing gloves or washing your hands after touching the peppers. Drop the habanero slices into a resealable glass container and fill with the Tito's. Cover the container and let it sit in a cool, dark place for 30 minutes . . . or a week. What's hot for some isn't hot for others, so we'll leave that timeline up to you. Strain out the peppers when the infusion reaches desired flavor and heat index. We suggest sticking it in the freezer before serving. Store in the freezer for up to 1 month, or in a cool, dark place for up to 2 weeks.

FIRESTARTER

Another way to cool down your drink? Sweeten it up with mango and top it with mint. Even the folks who prefer their orders mild and call ketchup "spicy" will enjoy this one.

———— ★ ————

The sharpness from the habanero is rounded out with the addition of cool, juicy mango. Mint, to top it all off, mellows the overall taste and makes for a smoother sip. By opting for tonic instead of sparkling water, you're adding a fourth component to your drink: bitterness.

3 fresh mint leaves
1½ ounces habanero-infused Tito's Handmade Vodka
½ ounce simple syrup (page 159)
1½ ounces mango juice
¼ ounce tonic water
1 fresh mint sprig, for garnish
1 lemon slice, for garnish

Muddle the mint leaves, infused Tito's, and simple syrup in a shaker, then strain into a glass with ice. Add the mango juice, stir, and top it off with tonic. Garnish with the mint sprig and lemon slice.

NO TIME FOR AN INFUSION? *Slice a habanero, remove the pith and seeds, muddle it in your glass, top with Tito's. Strain if desired.*

SWEET PEPPER INFUSION & SWEET PEPPER PALOMA

If you really, *really* are not into spice, that's okay. Swap the peppers that hit high on the Scoville scale for a sweet variety. You don't even need a freezer for this one.

SWEET PEPPER INFUSION

10 small sweet peppers
750 mL Tito's Handmade Vodka

Slice the peppers and remove the seeds before adding to a resealable glass
container. Fill with the Tito's, cover, and let it sit for 5 days, out of direct sunlight.
Taste-test and strain out the peppers when the infusion reaches desired flavor.
Store in a cool, dark place for up to 2 weeks.

SWEET PEPPER PALOMA

A tequila-based classic
made with Tito's: the
Sweet Pepper Paloma.
We're already
adding a twist here
by, ya know, using
vodka instead of the
traditional tequila. But,
hey, what's another one
for good measure? Hot
peppers in a cocktail are
standard, so give it a try
with something sweeter.

————— ★ —————

Sweet pepper's earthiness is subdued by grapefruit
and brightened with fresh mint.

> 1½ ounces sweet pepper–infused Tito's
> Handmade Vodka
> 1 ounce fresh grapefruit juice
> ½ ounce fresh lime juice
> ¼ ounce simple syrup (page 159)
> 3 ounces sparkling water
> 1 fresh mint sprig, for garnish

Add the infused Tito's, grapefruit juice, lime juice,
and simple syrup to a shaker with ice. Shake and
strain into a glass with fresh ice. Top with the
sparkling water and garnish with a mint sprig.

NO TIME FOR AN INFUSION? *Slice a sweet pepper, remove the pith and
seeds, muddle it in your glass, top with Tito's. Strain if desired.*

STRAWBERRY-HERB INFUSION & SIMPLE STRAWBERRY

Based on the rowdy debate that happened during the creation of this infusion, we've determined that cilantro is, without question, the most controversial herb in the garden.

We already knew that strawberry would be a hit. It's a team favorite that goes well in just about any cocktail. We also knew this classic could be elevated with fresh-picked herbs, adding an aromatic element to balance out the sweet.

But then there's the whole cilantro situation. Of course, you've got the "it tastes like soap" camp, the "I could eat a handful raw" camp, and the "it's fine" camp. So we threw in basil as an option, and you can decide what works best. Better yet? Host a taste test just like we did.

NO TIME FOR AN INFUSION?
*Slice 2 strawberries,
muddle them with your
choice of herb in a glass,
top with Tito's. Strain
if desired.*

STRAWBERRY-HERB INFUSION

16 ounces strawberries, hulled
5 fresh basil leaves or 5 fresh cilantro sprigs
750 mL Tito's Handmade Vodka

If you have time, slice the strawberries, and freeze them for a few hours (page 156). Then drop the strawberries into a resealable glass container with your choice of herb. Top with the Tito's, cover the container, and let it sit in the refrigerator for 5 to 7 days. Once the desired flavor is reached, strain out the fruit and herbs. Store in the refrigerator for up to 1 week.

SIMPLE STRAWBERRY

Like we said, any of these infusions only need a splash of sparkling or tonic water to make a cocktail. But strawberry's our favorite. It's simple, sweet, and looks very impressive.

★

Berries carry a natural sweetness that pairs perfectly with the herbal flavor of basil or cilantro. Basil offers rich, almost spiced, notes, giving the cocktail more depth. Cilantro carries a more lemony flavor, creating a lighter cocktail that plays up the tart elements found in the strawberry.

2 ounces strawberry herb–infused Tito's Handmade Vodka
Splash of sparkling or tonic water, optional

This can be served two ways. Shake up the infusion with ice and strain into a martini glass, or pour the infusion and your preferred bubbles into a glass with ice and stir.

FRUIT SALAD INFUSION & PICNIC POUR

Life's a picnic when there's vodka in your fruit salad. The best part about this belle of the barbecue is that there's really no recipe, even though we still give you one.

No matter how you slice it, every fruit salad is different. Homemade, prepackaged, even canned—there's always going to be variation, which means your infusion will always taste a little different.

So next time someone's hosting a backyard bash, volunteer to bring a side dish and show up with a jar of fruit salad–infused Tito's. It's more of a crowd-pleaser this way.

Tito's Tip

If you're using fruit with a thick skin (think citrus), remember to remove the pith. Otherwise, it'll make your cocktail bitter!

FRUIT SALAD INFUSION

2 cups fruit salad
2 cups Tito's Handmade Vodka

Add your favorite fruit salad to a resealable glass container and top with the
Tito's. Remember to remove the pith when using citrus (page 57). If you're going
prepackaged, we prefer fresh to canned. But if canned is your jam, just drain the
juice first (and maybe save it as a future mixer). Cover the container and refrigerate
it for 4 to 6 days, then strain out the fruit when the desired flavor is reached.
Freeze the leftover infused fruit to use as ice cubes. Store in the refrigerator for up
to 1 week.

PICNIC POUR

Sunny day, sunnier cocktail.

Crisp, bright, and just the right amount of fruity, this cocktail's got a little bit of everything for everyone at the picnic, barbecue, or any outdoor shindig.

———— ★ ————

Fruit, apple juice, and simple syrup mixed together make one sweet cocktail. By introducing tonic and lemon, the fruity flavors are toned down with much-needed bitterness. This cocktail is a reflection of whatever fruits you choose to include. If you're leaning toward a melon base, consider a little extra citrus to round out the flavor. Berry-forward? Consider fresh apples and pears to incorporate tart and spice.

> 2 ounces fruit salad–infused Tito's Handmade Vodka
> 1 ounce pressed apple juice
> ¼ ounce simple syrup (page 159)
> ¼ ounce fresh lemon juice
> 1 ounce tonic water
> Fresh fruit, for garnish

Add the infused Tito's, apple juice, simple syrup, and lemon juice to a shaker with ice. Shake and pour into a glass, top with more ice, and add the tonic water. Stir and spear a few pieces of fresh fruit as your garnish.

NO TIME FOR AN INFUSION? *Muddle whatever fruit ya got. Better yet, blend it. Then top with Tito's.*

TOASTED PECAN INFUSION & PECAN OLD FASHIONED

The coziest, warmest infusion you'll ever sip. Made for when there's a chill in the air, pecan pie in the oven, and you want to give someone a gift they'll actually use.

TOASTED PECAN INFUSION

1½ cups pecans, unsalted
750 mL Tito's Handmade Vodka

Preheat the oven to 350°F. Toast the pecans until they become aromatic, about 10 minutes. Let the pecans cool, drop them into a resealable glass container, and fill with the Tito's. Cover the container and let it sit for 3 to 4 weeks, out of direct sunlight . . . if you can wait that long. Strain out the pecans when the desired flavor is reached. Store in a cool, dark place for up to 1 month.

PECAN OLD FASHIONED

People might think you're a little out there for putting vodka in an old fashioned. Vodka . . . in an old fashioned? Can you blame them? Funny enough, the folks at Tito's have been questioned just the same. So much so, there was an intervention or two in the early days to talk us out of . . . well . . . keeping this whole thing going (because no one thought a Texas vodka would beat the imports).

It was the fishing trip that turned into "this vodka company is going to crash and burn; why don't you come work for me at the hardware shop?"

Then the job offer that turned into "wait, you're leaving a stable job in the spirits industry to work for a no-name brand that hasn't made a profit?"

Or the quick "you're too smart to be wasting the prime of your life on this" comment.

And a handful of similar stories after that.

If we've learned anything, though, it's that some of the best ideas are a little out of the ordinary, risky, against the norm. They might start with a list

(recipe continues)

you made when you couldn't sleep. They might gain traction when you find an old Dr Pepper keg at a junkyard. They might even succeed after a decade or two of trying. Just because they sound like they might not work when you first said them out loud doesn't mean they won't become something incredible.

Just like this drink.

The flavor here may not be from a barrel-aged batch, but roasting pecans creates a similar smoky effect. With a bitter exterior and a smooth, slightly sweet interior, the pecan infusion carries rich notes in every sip. With the hints of molasses found in brown sugar and just a slight spritz of citrus, our twist on a classic is nutty in all the right ways.

> 1 or 2 brown sugar cubes or 1 to 2 teaspoons brown sugar
> 3 dashes of orange bitters
> 2 ounces toasted pecan–infused Tito's Handmade Vodka
> 1 orange peel, for garnish

Muddle the sugar cubes and bitters directly in your glass. Add the infused Tito's and one large ice cube. Stir with a bar spoon and garnish with the orange peel after giving it a twist directly over your drink.

NO TIME FOR AN INFUSION? *Swap the brown sugar for pecan simple syrup (page 163) and top with Tito's.*

COFFEE INFUSION & AUSTIN ROAST

Here's why the Tito's Coffee Infusion makes the perfect gift.

You're invited to a housewarming in a few weeks. You might be the type to immediately go out and get the ingredients for a delicious coffee infusion to pair with custom glasses and a handwritten note about how to mix up a coffee-infused cocktail.

Or you might forget about the invitation entirely until three hours before the party starts. So you toss the ingredients into whatever jar you've got and scrawl some instructions about when it'll be ready to strain and sip. Boom. It's almost like two gifts: when you give it and when it's ready for them to drink it.

Either way, you can't lose with this one.

COFFEE INFUSION

2 vanilla bean pods
750 mL Tito's Handmade Vodka
1 cup ground coffee
1 to 2 cups simple syrup (page 159)

Slice open the vanilla bean pods and add to a resealable glass container. Pour in the Tito's, coffee, and simple syrup. Add more or less syrup, depending on how sweet you like your coffee. Our suggestion is to start with 1 cup of simple syrup; you can always make it sweeter. Cover the container and let it sit in a cool, dark place for 2 weeks, shaking occasionally. The flavor gets even better after a month or so . . . if you can be patient. Strain the infusion through a fine sifter until the coffee grounds are removed. Store in a cool, dark place for up to 2 weeks.

AUSTIN ROAST

It's Tito's Espresso Martini meets iced coffee from the café down the street—you know, the one you told yourself you'd stop getting every morning, but it's so much better than the cold brew in your fridge—meets a chocolate orange.

It's an Austin Roast.

────── ★ ──────

Why does the chocolate orange sell out during holiday season? Because chocolate and orange go really well together. Now, take it one step further: a mocha latte, another instance of sweetness and acidity coming together. The Austin Roast is all about balancing these two counterparts to achieve a smooth sip that's reminiscent of a few of our favorite things. If you like your cup of joe on the lighter side, add a splash of your choice of creamer; we prefer half-and-half.

1½ ounces coffee-infused Tito's Handmade Vodka
1 ounce cold brew
½ ounce crème de cacao
½ ounce half-and-half, optional
1 orange slice (about ¼ ounce)

Add the infused Tito's, cold brew, crème de cacao, and half-and-half (if using) to a glass with ice, squeeze the orange slice 'til there's nothing left, and stir.

NO TIME FOR AN INFUSION? *Add 1 extra ounce of cold brew and a splash of simple syrup, then top with Tito's.*

BEET INFUSION & GOOD ROOTS

Introducing the most beautiful infusion that's worth the stained fingers. Sure, not everyone is a fan of vegetables in their vodka, but the slightly sweet, earthy notes of fresh beets and their deep garnet color may persuade you. And don't worry, rinsing your hands with lemon juice or a baking soda and water mixture should get those stains right out.

NO TIME FOR AN INFUSION? *Swap the infusion for 1½ ounces beet juice and 1½ ounces Tito's.*

BEET INFUSION

3 beets
750 mL Tito's Handmade Vodka

Clean, peel, and chop beets into cubes—no need to cook 'em; raw is fine. Place them in a resealable glass container and fill with Tito's. Cover the container, shake it up, and store in a cool, dark place for 5 days, shaking the infusion daily. Strain out the beets when the infusion has reached the desired flavor. Store in a cool, dark place for up to 5 days.

GOOD ROOTS

The most beautiful infusions make the most beautiful cocktails. The next time you host a farm-to-table soirée or actually wake up early enough to get to the farmer's market and finally cook that locally grown kale, make sure this drink is on the menu.

———— ★ ————

Beets may be earthy (look where they grow), but pair them with honey and their own natural sweetness shines through. Another one of our favorite root vegetables, ginger, adds a nice level of spice to the normally mellow tone of beets. Top it off with citrus and mint to brighten it all up.

> 2 ounces beet-infused Tito's Handmade Vodka
> 1 ounce ginger-honey syrup (page 161)
> 1 ounce fresh lemon juice
> 3 fresh mint sprigs

Add the infused Tito's, ginger-honey syrup, lemon juice, and 2 mint sprigs to a shaker with ice. Shake and strain into a glass. Garnish with the remaining mint sprig.

BLACK CHERRY INFUSION
& THE SHACK SPRITZ

As our dream slowly became a reality, we needed a place to set up shop—a place that didn't cost much and where late-night activity wouldn't bother anyone but the cicadas.

Enter: The Shack.

It started with a plot of land on the outskirts of Southeast Austin, a few acres just inside the city limits. The clay soil was cracked, tumbleweeds rolled by unironically, and it was cheap enough. We picked a point, grabbed a shovel, and broke ground.

We built the frame and poured the foundation, meticulously mimicking the methods used in military barracks. To this day, the concrete doesn't have a single crack. After that, the walls went up, the roof rolled out, and an old cot was thrown in the back for those late nights.

At 998 square feet, the Shack stood just shy of permit requirements. Hey, we were still getting the lay of the land.

What does all of this have to do with cherries?

When things were up and running and the recipe was in a good spot, we made our first-ever infusion with our very own vodka.

The Tito's Black Cherry Infusion.

To this day, it still sits on a shelf alongside old photos, bottles from over the years, and a few other relics of Tito's past.

BLACK CHERRY INFUSION

20 black cherries or ½ cup dried cherries
750 mL Tito's Handmade Vodka

Roasting your own cherries is well worth it, but sometimes there aren't enough hours in the day and we get that. If you do want to give homemade a try, remove the pits from your fresh cherries (poking a metal straw through the center should do the trick), slice them in half, and roast them in the oven at 150°F for 10 to 12 hours, until they are sweet and jammy.

Once they're ready, put them in a resealable glass container and fill to the top with Tito's. If you're using dried, do the same. Cover the container and let it sit for 3 to 5 days. Strain out the cherries when the infusion has reached the desired flavor. Store in a cool, dark place for up to 1 month.

THE SHACK SPRITZ

In the early days, before Tito's, black cherry was actually our most requested infusion. Every now and then, a few raspberries would be added to the mix for an extra splash of tart and sweet, making the fan favorite an even bigger hit.

Infusions are all about experimenting, so feel free to follow suit and sneak a few raspberries into your infusion too. Then turn that infusion into a spritz, and toast to all the best moments, especially the ones that make you feel like you've made it.

———— ★ ————

We took cues from a fine red wine and an aged port, then added some sparkle, capturing the spirit of a celebratory toast or an after-dinner drink. Unlike those wines, we use citrus to bring out the natural tartness of cherry juice and turned something decadent into a lighter spritz.

> 1 ounce black cherry–infused Tito's Handmade Vodka
> ½ ounce orange liqueur
> ¼ ounce fresh lime juice
> 2 ounces sparkling white wine, chilled
> 1 lime twist, for garnish

Add the infused Tito's, orange liqueur, and lime juice to a shaker with ice and give it a shake. Strain into a flute, top with your bubbles, and garnish with the lime twist.

NO TIME FOR AN INFUSION? *Muddle fresh, pitted cherries and top with Tito's. Strain if desired.*

AUSTIN &
TEXAS

Texas Born and Raised

We built Texas's first legal operating distillery on twelve acres of land in Southeast Austin, which was bought with a credit card check and financed through the seller.

Pull up a seat at your favorite bar. Order your usual, chat with the bartender, and swap a story or two with the friend—or stranger— sitting next to you.

There's something about finding your seat at the table or, in this case, the bar top. It's that sense of place after a long week, that familiar nod or wave when you head inside, the confident "This is the spot" when asked "Where's a good place to get a drink?"

As soon as the vodka was ready, Tito's started looking for that seat—making our way through crowded bars, restaurants with no open tables, liquor stores that closed up shop every time we tried to walk through the door (metaphorically speaking).

But somewhere along the way, Austin made space and invited Tito's to sit down.

Our hometown may not have paved the way for immediate success—we'd have to get there on our own—but it set the scene for us to keep going every time the going got tough.

And most of the time, the going was pretty tough.

But it was those local establishments—the ones that tried our vodka and listened to our story—that made the hard work worth it. They didn't see us for our stock bottle, our rough edges, or the fact that we always showed up to business meetings with dogs. They saw us for our spirit.

We owe everything to the city where our vodka started and continues to live today, and especially to the Austin locals who gave us a shot and pulled up a seat.

THE MOCKINGBIRD

When we surveyed the land for our distillery, a desolate plot in far-out Southeast Austin, we spotted a tree that seemed to be singing, its branches filled with mockingbirds. All that dust surrounded by nothing could have deterred this whole operation, but now we had an ornithological good omen telling us we were headed in the right direction.

We bought the property that day.

It's called Mockingbird Distillery, an ode to Texas's state bird that showed us where we were meant to be.

---- ★ ----

Consider this cocktail a bouquet of floral notes: lavender, violet, and elderflower blending together to create an aroma-forward drink. On their own, these three elements can taste slightly perfumy, but cut with herbal dry vermouth and acid from the lemon twist, those notes become well-rounded for a balanced and bright sip.

> 2 ounces Tito's Handmade Vodka
> ½ ounce dry vermouth
> ½ ounce elderflower liqueur
> ¼ ounce violet liqueur
> 1 dash of lavender bitters
> 1 lemon twist, for garnish

Add the Tito's, vermouth, elderflower liqueur, violet liqueur, and lavender bitters to a shaker with ice. Shake and strain into a martini glass. Garnish with the lemon twist.

The original Mockingbird Distillery sign

THE GRACKLE

Enter the mockingbird's aggressive cousin with an extra-spicy personality: the grackle.

They're not actually cousins—the grackle looks more like a crow and acts like a seagull. But they are both well-known Texas locals with reputations that precede them.

Grackles have been invading al fresco dinners, picnics, and drinks on the patio since the mid-1800s, when they invaded the state of Texas and never left. Their metallic black feathers and cold yellow eyes have become a staple of our city. You're not a real Austinite until a grackle has cackled in your direction or stolen a tortilla chip when you weren't looking.

They've got attitude and a presence that, while at times frightening, is commendable. The grackle has made a name for itself in Austin, and across Texas, out of sheer determination, a refusal to give up, and a song that resembles a car alarm. Sound familiar (aside from the car alarm part)?

We may not love 'em, but we respect 'em. At least enough to make a drink in their honor.

This is a mean cocktail, just like its namesake. The spicy jalapeño and tart yet sweet blackberries are good friends; they complement each other's flavor profiles and mellow any overwhelming heat or sugar. Adding aromatic bitters and a hint of citrus creates dynamic layers and a balanced finish.

2 fresh jalapeño slices (page 156), plus 1 extra for garnish, optional
5 blackberries
1½ ounces Tito's Handmade Vodka
½ ounce simple syrup (page 159)

2 dashes of orange bitters
2 dashes of herbal bitters
1 dash of fresh lime juice
1 lime wheel, for garnish, optional

Muddle 2 jalapeño slices, the blackberries, and the Tito's in a shaker. Add the simple syrup, orange bitters, herbal bitters, and lime juice and give it a shake. Toss in a handful of ice, shake it one more time, and strain into a martini glass. Garnish with the remaining jalapeño slice and a lime wheel, if desired.

SMOKED PEACH MULE

"You haven't had barbecue until you've had Texas barbecue."

—TEXANS EVERYWHERE

"You haven't had vodka until you've had Texas vodka." —US

"You haven't had peaches until you've had Texas peaches."

—TEXANS EVERYWHERE, US, AND TEXAS PEACH FARMERS (WE ASSUME)

There are a few things Texas does really well. Vodka and barbecue are two of them. And they go together quite nicely.

When Tito's was ready to hit the shelves, we made our way to spots across Austin, asking local bar and restaurant owners to give us a try. We knew that if they liked what they tasted, they'd encourage their customers to give us a try too. Sure, we hit the expected places—cocktail bars, dives, and restaurants that knew how to make a mean vodka martini—but we didn't stop there. Tequila bars? Sure. Barbecue joints? You bet.

Thankfully, a lot of them liked our product and agreed to add a few bottles to the bar.

One of the first was the County Line, known for its legendary barbecue. They liked Tito's so much, in fact, we got some free brisket the day our copper cap hit the backbar, and we've held a permanent place there ever since.

And then there are peaches.

If you combine this Texan trifecta in a copper mug, the end result will be a real treat.

When you sear a juicy peach on the grill, you're not only caramelizing its natural sugars, but the char alters the fruit's flavor, making it smoky and savory.

(recipe continues)

The ginger brings the heat, the lime checks the box for citrus, and in one sip you have a perfectly balanced combination of core flavor profiles: sweet, savory, spicy, and acidic.

1 peach, halved and pitted

1 lime, halved

1¾ ounces Tito's Handmade Vodka

3 ounces ginger beer

Fire up the grill. (If you don't have a grill, use a cast-iron skillet or any frying pan over high heat.) Start by searing your peach and lime halves, flesh side down. Once they've got a nice char, remove and cut the peach halves into thin slices. Place two peach slices and one lime half into a Tito's Copper Mug and muddle. Add ice, the Tito's, and ginger beer. Stir and garnish with a grilled peach slice.

HERE ARE A FEW PLACES TO GET BARBECUE NEXT TIME YOU'RE IN AUSTIN:

B. Cooper Barbeque

Black's Barbecue

Brown's Bar-B-Que

Cooper's Old Time Pit
  Bar-B-Que

The County Line

Distant Relatives

Franklin Barbecue

H-E-B (yes, it's at a
  grocery store)

KG BBQ

InterStellar BBQ

Iron Works Barbecue

la Barbecue

Lamberts

LeRoy and Lewis Barbecue

Loro

Micklethwait Craft Meats

Mum Foods

Rollin Smoke BBQ

Salt Lick BBQ

Sam's Bar-B-Que

SLAB BBQ & Beer

Stiles Switch BBQ & Brew

Stubb's Bar-B-Q

Terry Black's Barbecue

Valentina's Tex Mex BBQ

Whitfield's

Road-tripping to Austin? You can always stop at Buc-ee's.

BAT-TINI

Austin's got some well-known birds, but they're not the only winged icons of our city. We've also got bats. Millions and millions of Mexican free-tailed bats.

A bat colony turned the South Congress Bridge into home sweet home, and at every sunset during the hotter months, folks gather round to watch them take flight in search of dinner. It's one of our biggest tourist attractions. There are watch parties, people sell novelty items, boat rentals take out-of-towners on the water for a front-row seat directly underneath the bridge.

Bats are such a big deal here that, in 2010, Tito's sponsored Austin's Best Bat-Tini Competition. Bars across the city entered to shake up their most creative, and delicious, Tito's cocktail inspired by our beloved bats.

The Driskill Hotel took first place.

This cocktail is meant to be refreshing and simple yet complex enough to be considered an elevated libation. We think this hits the mark. Hibiscus not only offers beautiful color, but it has a sweet scent and subtle flavor as well. By adding the spice from ginger and the acid from citrus, those flavors become louder and brighter without overwhelming the senses.

1½ ounces Tito's Handmade Vodka
½ ounce fresh lemon juice
½ ounce fresh lime juice
¼ ounce agave nectar

½ ounce hibiscus-ginger syrup (page 161)
1 blackberry, for garnish
1 hibiscus flower, for garnish

Add the Tito's, lemon juice, lime juice, agave, and hibiscus-ginger syrup to a shaker with ice. Shake and strain into a chilled martini glass or a glass with fresh ice. Garnish with the blackberry and hibiscus flower.

FIRE IN THE HOLE

Every time our bottle found a home on a new backbar, a friendship formed.

One as strong as they come was found with Kevin Williamson, Austin legend and late owner of one of our team's go-to spots, Ranch 616.

When he first came across Tito's, he did more than agree to sell our vodka. He created a standout shooter and put it on his menu. Because that's the sort of thing that Kevin did. He didn't just agree to have dinner, he cooked you a four-course meal himself. And he didn't just try Tito's, he hollowed out a jalapeño, poured in a shot, and yelled, "Fire in the hole!"

We loved it so much, we made a thousand of those suckers a year or so later, huddled up in a hotel room in New Orleans while cohosting a party with none other than Kevin himself. An assembly line of Tito's folks worked to hollow out crates of jalapeños, taking each pepper one by one and prepping them for the event.

Until hotel guests started complaining.

Eyes watered, throats burned, an aroma that made it hard to breathe wafted through hallways and down to the lobby.

A note for next time: cut the peppers outside.

The Fire in the Hole has become a badge of honor. It was named the Official Drink of Austin in 2008 and again in 2009. To this day, new Tito's team members are welcomed with this two-tiered concoction. It's another one of those "unofficial, official" cocktails we've grown to love and one that we'll forever raise to Kevin Williamson of Ranch 616.

Imagine biting into a TitoRita (page 35). This drink is kind of like that, except now you have a new element: heat. Before this cocktail scares you off, note that the jalapeño's sting is subdued with the addition of orange liqueur and citrus juice. Its rim, packed with spices, boosts the overall profile, working as a magnifying glass to bring those flavors to life.

1 jalapeño
Salt, chile powder, crushed red pepper, and cayenne for the rim (page 5)

1 ounce Tito's Handmade Vodka
1 ounce orange liqueur
1 ounce fresh lime juice

Start by removing the top of the jalapeño and hollowing the jalapeño out with a sharp knife, discarding the pith and seeds. Either use gloves or wash your hands a few times after you're done. Once your jalapeño is good to go, dip the rim into your spice mixture. (We suggest 1 part salt, ¾ part chile powder, ½ part crushed red pepper, and ¼ part cayenne. Eyeballing it is just fine too.) Place your jalapeño upright in a small glass. Add the Tito's, orange liqueur, and lime juice to a shaker with ice. Give it a shake, then carefully strain it into your jalapeño, letting it pour over the side into your glass.

You might think you're done, but there's something to how you drink this one.

Step 1: Raise your pepper.
Step 2: Drink it up.

Step 3: Take a bite of the pepper.
Step 4: Enjoy whatever's left in your glass.

LAKE BREAKFAST

Austin's got one hell of a lake culture. Lady Bird Lake (or Town Lake depending on when you moved to Austin) is the center of the city. It's ten miles of trail running through downtown, usually packed with kayakers and paddleboarders. As you head west and the skyscrapers become suburbs, the more tranquil Lake Austin opens up into the Texas Hill Country with boats docked at a few favorite lakeside dives, coffee shops, and restaurants. On the edge of Travis County lies Lake Travis, the "lake" that actually looks and acts like one. Double the size of Lady Bird and Lake Austin combined, Lake Travis is where you'll find solace or a party on any given summer weekend.

Point is, we love our lakes.

They're the watering holes that bring folks together when the days are sweltering and the nights aren't much cooler. We pack up our paddles, our shades, and our preferred beverages, then hit the cool blue all before brunch.

Because the next best way to beat the heat is to start early. So let's do breakfast.

Blueberry pancakes and bacon go really, really well together. Salty bacon pairs perfectly with maple syrup. Cut with tart blueberry, everything instantly brightens up. It's cocktail science.

> 1 ounce Tito's Handmade Vodka
> 1 ounce maple simple syrup (page 162)
> 1 ounce blueberry juice
> 1 piece of crispy bacon

Pour the Tito's and maple simple syrup into a glass. Pour the blueberry juice into a second glass. Get your piece of bacon ready. Raise a toast and drink your maple and Tito's sipper. Follow up with the blueberry juice. Finish off with a bite of bacon.

TEXAS SIPPER

One of our most refreshing summer cocktails was created at a boat party.

The team had become big fans of Jack Allen's Kitchen, a local spot known for its southern comfort food and strong Austin spirit. It put Tito's on the menu and added fresh grapefruit, elderflower, and sage. Tart, crisp, slightly aromatic. There's a reason this one became a favorite.

Fast-forward to being in the middle of Lake Travis with a jug of grapefruit juice, some sparkling water, and, well, yes, some elderflower liqueur. We are in the industry, after all. We used mint instead of sage, and the Tito's Texas Sipper was born, forever an ode to its original.

On their own, grapefruit and elderflower are strong flavors. Combined, they form a bond, toning down the bitter citrus and floral sweetness to create cocktail harmony. Activated with bubbles, smoothed out with Tito's, and energized with just a hint of mint, this combination is tried and true.

>   2 ounces fresh grapefruit juice
>   1½ ounces Tito's Handmade Vodka
>   ½ ounce elderflower liqueur
>   1 ounce sparkling water
>   1 fresh mint sprig, for garnish

Add the grapefruit juice, Tito's, and elderflower liqueur to a shaker with ice. Shake and strain into a glass with fresh ice and top with the sparkling water. Now, it might sound strange, but slap your mint sprig between your palms to release those natural oils and bring out its refreshing aroma. Then toss it on top.

LONE STARDUST

Tito's: the official spirit of Texas.

Lone Star: the official beer of Texas.

Just makes sense to try 'em out together.

──────── ★ ────────

Summer punch, a batch of shandies, river daze. Whatever you call it, we can all agree that pink lemonade and beer taste like a sunny day in the middle of July. Hops aren't for everyone, but with a light enough brew, chilled Tito's, and a splash of bubbles, the flavor becomes crisp and refreshing.

BATCH

12 ounces Tito's Handmade Vodka

12 ounces Lone Star beer or your preferred light domestic beer

12 ounces water

12 ounces frozen pink lemonade concentrate, thawed

12 ounces sparkling water

3 lemons, sliced

Add the Tito's, beer, water, pink lemonade concentrate, sparkling water, and 2 sliced lemons to a gallon pitcher and stir to combine. For each drink, pour 6 to 10 ounces of the mixture into a glass with ice. Garnish with the remaining lemon slices. Serves 6 to 12.

PARTY THE SIZE OF TEXAS

Two 750 mL bottles of Tito's Handmade Vodka

48 ounces Lone Star beer or your preferred light domestic beer

48 ounces water

48 ounces frozen pink lemonade concentrate, thawed

48 ounces sparkling water

12 lemons, sliced

Repeat the above directions in a much larger vessel, reserving 4 of the sliced lemons for garnishing the glasses. Serves 30 to 40.

THE AFTER PARTY

You've made it through bats and boat parties, barbecue and jalapeño shooters, dive-bombing grackles, and a sprinkle of Lone Stardust.

We know there's no better place to raise one than Austin, Texas, so when you need to cleanse your palate after a night or two in the city that raised us, go for something simple that still captures our hometown spirit.

Hey, just because it's "after" doesn't mean it's not a party.

———— ★ ————

Call it a Tito's Mule Lite. By combining ginger beer with sparkling water, the spice of the ginger is mellowed and becomes a subtle background element, allowing fresh citrus to be the star.

> 2 ounces Tito's Handmade Vodka
> 2 ounces sparkling water
> 2 ounces ginger beer
> ½ ounce citrus juice (lime, lemon, or orange—choose your own adventure)

Add everything to a glass with ice and stir. Yep, that's it.

SOUNDS
& STAGES

You know that friend—the musician, the artist, the poet—who invites you to every set, gallery, or dimly lit café to see them show the world everything they've got? You might not have that friend because you might be that friend. But if you're not, you're probably the one supporting. The one who pays the cover. Shares the flyer. Shows up at 10 P.M. on a Tuesday and buys them a drink after the stage goes dark. Ready to do it all again next month because you believe in them.

Tito's is that one, the second friend.

While we were getting our start, we watched the city around us fill with working musicians starting out just the same, sharing the same circles; our Austin experience overlapped somewhere between drinks and mic stands. We loved every second of it. Still do. The energy, the grit, the good music, and the spirit.

Since those earliest days, we've supported local musicians in every way that we could. From grungy dives, with punk-band leads turning bar tops to stages, to

TITO'S HANDMADE VODKA AT AUSTIN CITY LIMITS
EST. 2002

THE FIRST AUSTIN CITY LIMITS MUSIC FESTIVAL WAS HELD IN 2002, RIGHT HERE IN ZILKER PARK. TITO'S HANDMADE VODKA JOINED THE FUN IN 2003, BACK WHEN R.E.M. AND AL GREEN HEADLINED. TITO BEVERIDGE, FOUNDER & MASTER DISTILLER OF TITO'S HANDMADE VODKA AND DEVOTED MUSIC FAN, WORKED BY HIMSELF THAT YEAR, POURING SAMPLES, MIXING DRINKS (THE TITO'S SWEET-O WAS ONE OF THE FIRST ACL COCKTAILS), AND SPREADING THE WORD ABOUT THE VODKA THAT HE WAS DISTILLING RIGHT DOWN THE ROAD.

THROUGH THE YEARS, TITO'S HANDMADE VODKA HAS CONTINUED TO PLAY A CRUCIAL ROLE IN THE AUSTIN CITY LIMITS FESTIVAL EXPERIENCE FOR ARTISTS AND VIP ATTENDEES. IN 2015, TITO'S HANDMADE VODKA HAD A DEDICATED STAGE FOR THE VERY FIRST TIME, A PLINKO PARLOR IN GENERAL ADMISSION FEATURING FUN FESTIVAL PRIZES, AND EVEN CREATED A TITO'S LOUNGE, A MID-FESTIVAL OASIS FOR THE COMPANY'S FAMILY AND FRIENDS. THE PARTNERSHIP BETWEEN THESE TWO AUSTIN ORIGINALS CONTINUES TO EVOLVE EVEN TODAY. TITO'S HANDMADE VODKA IS A PROUD SPONSOR OF THE AUSTIN CITY LIMITS MUSIC FESTIVAL AND THE THRIVING SPIRIT OF MUSIC THAT LIVES ON IN AUSTIN, TEXAS.

honky-tonks, with two-step stomping and live country pouring out the windows, Tito's was showing up.

As we got bigger and could do more, we did. We began working with nonprofits dedicated to helping musicians and ingrained ourselves in the fabric of iconic local haunts. We started showing up outside of Austin too, forging new connections with folks in the music industry, from artists to crew to the bartenders mixing drinks during opening acts.

It was a lot of being in the right place at the right time, but the Austin music scene wove itself into our culture and shaped who we are: fans at heart, always ready to keep the drinks flowing and the show going.

THE OPENING ACT

Ever go to see your favorite band and leave thinking more about the opening act than the headliner? You'd never heard of them, but now you're deep into their discography and buying tickets for their next show.

Tito's was like the opening act for craft spirits. Our name may have been undiscovered, but once people heard our story and gave us a try, they stuck with us.

The best part of becoming a new fan, of a band or a drink, is sharing what you love. It's more than being the person who heard it first; it's the thrill of finding the other folks who want to hear it too.

———— ★ ————

Maybe you'll find fellow Creamsicle fans, and then you'll both be in for a treat. The orange flavor in the sour mix mimics the flavor of everyone's favorite ice cream on a stick. The citrus is instantly cooled down with the creamy flavor found in vanilla and simple syrup.

> 3 ounces Tito's Handmade Vodka
> 2 ounces sour mix
> ½ ounce simple syrup (page 159)
> 1 teaspoon vanilla extract
> 1 lemon slice, for garnish

Add the Tito's, sour mix, simple syrup, and vanilla to a shaker with ice. Shake and strain into a glass with fresh ice. Garnish with the lemon slice.

DOWN ON DIRTY

The entire city of Austin is full of live music, but there's something different about Dirty.

Known to Austinites as Dirty 6th or just Dirty for short, 6th Street was once deemed "The Street of Dreams"—a road paved with opportunity. Even though the nickname has changed, the opportunity is still there. (It was also called Pecan Street at one point.) Musicians cram into corner stages at every pub, dive, and two-story bar, playing their hearts out and getting their sound into the world. Everything from psychedelic garage rock to '90s-inspired DJs to indie vocalists backed by a single guitar spills out of windows and doorways that line the street, while locals and out-of-towners pop in and out, some leaving with a new band to follow.

Tito's got a taste of that opportunity, in a way—walking into bars along 6th Street before business hours, telling our story with a bottle in tow. It may have been dirty, but it was the place for big dreams, and we had a case full of 'em.

Plus, when it comes to cocktails, some say the dirtier the better.

This cocktail captures the salty, briny flavor you love in a dirty martini but adds a few new layers. Celery juice cuts the brine with a subtle sweetness. By adding in a few drops of hot sauce, natural heat heightens each chilled sip. We suggest biting into your peperoncino to add a touch more salt and heat before your glass is empty.

2 ounces Tito's Handmade Vodka
1 ounce olive brine
½ ounce celery juice
3 to 5 dashes of hot sauce, to taste

3 green or pimento-stuffed olives, for garnish
1 peperoncino pepper, for garnish

Add the Tito's, olive brine, celery juice, and hot sauce to a shaker with ice. Shake and strain into a martini glass. Make a little kebab with your olives and peperoncino on a toothpick or short skewer and toss it on top.

CHARRED VINYL

Our love of music spans stages and venues, but it can also be found in stacks and crates. The nostalgic simplicity of sipping drinks and spinning vinyl isn't lost on us, and it plays as a nice reminder of our earliest days.

For a long time, Tito's has sponsored a limited-edition vinyl release—a compilation featuring tracks from a record label's catalog selected by folks who work in record stores and curated by a music historian. It hits stores on the same day every year, a day we look forward to: Record Store Day.

Record Store Day celebrates independent record stores across the country, the brick-and-mortars that keep physical media alive by hosting listening parties and in-store shows, connecting fans to new artists and the tracks they love through a needle dropping and a record spinning.

On RSD, we pull out an album from the day's haul, mix up a smoky drink, and sit back to take it all in.

Rosemary on its own packs a sensory punch with its strong aroma. Torching it transforms the herb, bringing out its woodsy qualities of pine and pepper. Those flavor notes are enhanced with fresh citrus, and the cocktail is sweetened with ginger beer for a smoky yet easy-to-drink sipper.

2 fresh rosemary sprigs	3 ounces ginger beer
2 ounces Tito's Handmade Vodka	2 lemon slices, for garnish
½ ounce fresh lemon juice	1 lemon twist, for garnish

Torch 1 rosemary sprig using a butane torch (or a gas stovetop) until lightly charred and let cool. In a shaker with ice, add the Tito's, lemon juice, and 1 charred rosemary sprig. Shake and strain into a glass, then top with ginger beer and stir to combine. Spear the lemon slices with the remaining rosemary sprig and torch it. Submerge it into your drink and garnish with the lemon twist.

FEST SIPPER

Since 2002, musicians of all genres and levels of experience and recognition come to our hometown to play over the course of two weekends. Austin's Zilker Park transforms into a multistage open-air venue, with local restaurants-turned-food-booths ready and waiting for that between-set-snack as you wind your way from one end to the other.

In 2003, Tito's joined the festival grounds.

After ACL Fest's inaugural year, we knew a bunch of bands playing at Zilker was right up our alley. We'd never done anything like this before, and people were only just starting to hear about us, but a friend of a friend floated the idea and opened the door. We showed up like we always do and tended bar, shooting the breeze and comparing notes on the lineup while handing out our new festival cocktail: Tito's and sweet tea.

After sponsoring ACL Fest that year, we went on to work with more festivals across the country. Big or small, local or nationally recognized, we jump at the chance to pour some drinks, listen to a few songs, and swap stories while the next band sets up.

We've added more cocktails to the menu over the years, but there's nothing like sipping something inspired by our first.

Sweet tea is a Texas staple. Folks will argue how sweet it should really be and who makes the best batch, but we think it deserves a permanent spot in the fridge. The key to a great sweet tea is to make sure the tea isn't masked by sugar. Once you've got your perfect brew, a squeeze of fresh lemon brightens the flavor.

SWEET TEA INFUSION

3 black tea bags
3 cups Tito's Handmade Vodka
1 cup honey simple syrup (page 162)
4 to 5 tablespoons fresh lemon juice

To mix up your batch, start by steeping your black tea bags in the Tito's for 3 hours at room temperature in a resealable glass container. When your infusion is finished, remove the tea bags, squeezing out any leftover liquid. Stir in your honey simple syrup and lemon juice.

COCKTAIL

3 ounces sweet tea–infused Tito's Handmade Vodka
2 ounces sparkling water
1 lemon slice, for garnish

Add the infused Tito's to a glass with ice, top with sparkling water, and garnish with the lemon slice.

THE HEADLINER

We weren't sure where this whole thing would take us or how people would respond to a brand-new Texas vodka.

It took some time, but thanks to our fans, we went from playing local dives to headlining the main stage. Some would even call us a smash hit.

———— ★ ————

Green grapes and serrano chiles are an unexpected sweet and spicy combination. Their loud flavors are slightly muted by the addition of citrus and sugar, bringing a brightness to their bite. Smashing them all together isn't just a good time, it's a science; breaking down their physical barriers extracts the essence of each element. Call it the mosh pit of cocktails.

> 2 ounces Tito's Handmade Vodka
> 5 green grapes
> 1 serrano pepper, sliced (page 156)
> 1 lime slice
> 1 sugar cube or 1 teaspoon granulated sugar
> 1 dash of bitters

Muddle the Tito's, grapes, pepper slices (leaving one slice for the garnish, if desired), lime, sugar, and bitters in a shaker. Add ice and shake vigorously. Strain into a glass with fresh ice. Garnish with a slice of serrano if you want an extra kick.

When the music fades and the lights come on, how do you end your night?

NIGHTCAP

You're with the right person. Perched at a quiet, dimly lit corner table still buzzing from the show that just changed your entire perspective on music.

You clink your glasses in agreement and keep the night going.

———— ★ ————

A room-temperature cocktail is complex. It's bold and can't be masked or watered down by ice. The walnut liqueur has a warm, rich, nutty flavor with a hint of sharpness. Tito's, in contrast, lightens up that richness just the right amount. The final addition of a cherry adds depth, mimicking notes of aged port. It's a great last bite before you call it a night.

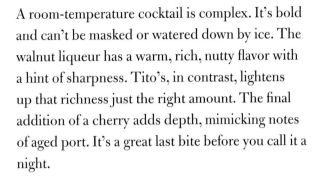

> 2 ounces Tito's Handmade Vodka
> 2 ounces walnut liqueur
> 1 gourmet cocktail cherry

Combine the Tito's and walnut liqueur in a shaker at room temperature; no need for ice in this one. Shake for 30 seconds or so, then pour into a glass. Spoon in a cherry with a little of its juice from the jar.

THE LAST BATCH

Someone's got the perfect post-show party playlist—a little '90s nostalgia, beats dropping, bass hitting. Everything's clicking and all your favorite people have wound up in one room. It's late-late but pizza still sounds good even if it's almost time for breakfast.

You raise your glasses to a night like no other and take a swig.

Four ingredients and a ton of flavor: The Last Batch. We don't typically mix Tito's with a dark cola, but when we do it right, it's delicious. Double up on cola's cinnamon and vanilla flavors with a cinnamon-vanilla syrup. Yes, it's sweet, but the almond liqueur adds a nutty bitterness that rounds out the overall flavor.

COCKTAIL

1 ounce Tito's Handmade Vodka

½ ounce almond liqueur

¾ cup cola

1 ounce cinnamon-vanilla simple syrup (page 160)

Fill a glass with ice, add all your ingredients, then stir.

PITCHER

½ cup Tito's Handmade Vodka

¼ cup almond liqueur

3 cups cola

¼ cup cinnamon-vanilla simple syrup (page 160)

See above but make that glass a pitcher. Serves 2 to 4.

LOVE & DOGS

How do you fill your cup? Metaphorically speaking, that is.

Once cases started selling and copper caps appeared on shelves across Austin, we asked ourselves that very question. Making vodka was the dream, but what if we could be bigger than the bottle? To distill spirits and raise them too? To give back to the community that built us up?

Well, as it happened, we could do just that. First, there was an impromptu nonprofit event, then the first few dog rescues, and eventually a regenerative farm for our very own team.

Turning spirits into love and goodness became the heart of Tito's Handmade Vodka.

LOVE, TITO'S

Our cups stay full because we found meaning and purpose in the work we do. We'd bring the life of the party and be the catalyst for a good time, but we'd also make a difference in the community where that party was being thrown.

Early on, after donating a few cases to local nonprofits, we started to figure out that Tito's could play a larger role in the world of giving back—sharing our vodka, making monetary donations, and showing up to volunteer. Purposeful action became part of who we are as a brand and as the individuals who make up the team.

Members of the Tito's team are encouraged to get involved with their own communities and the causes that mean something to them; Tito's will match, sponsor, and support every step of the way.

What began as individual, localized gestures became a worldwide movement comprised of service projects, sponsored nonprofit events, and a drive to show up wherever there's room to help.

Why do we call our program *Love, Tito's*? It's a simple signoff that says it all.

You take your passion,
mix it with community,
and that's your meaning
and purpose.

—TITOISM #12

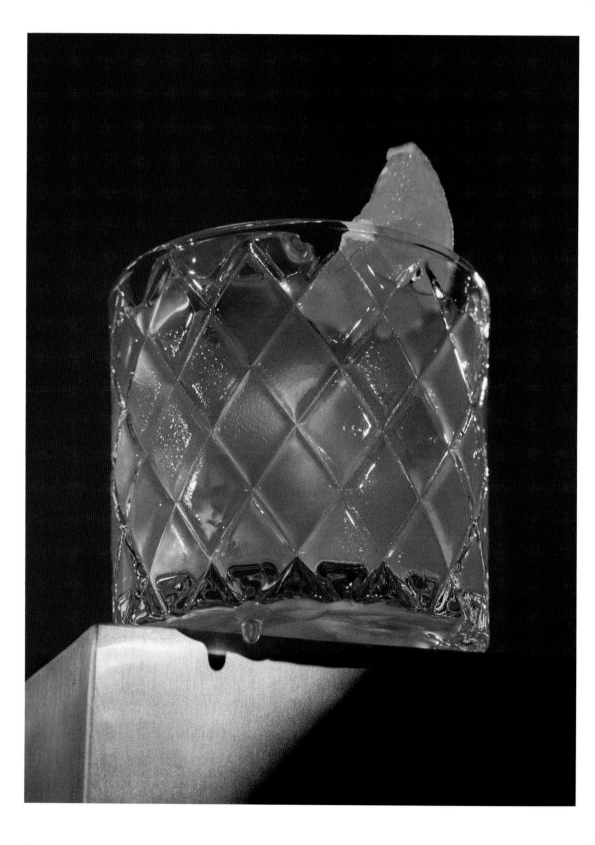

HEART & SOUL

The Tito's team is all too familiar with group outings, happy hours, and holiday parties.

But we've got a rule: Whenever twenty or more team members are together at one time, we try to participate in a charitable activity.

The activities are chosen to meet the needs of whatever neighborhood or city we're in—dog walking, beach clean-up, letter writing, disaster-relief kit making, or something else that's specific to that area. Tito's became Tito's because of the friends and fans who not only gave us a chance, but lent a hand whenever we needed it. We strive to give back and keep that momentum going, and then end the day with a celebratory cocktail.

Campari is an acquired taste. It's spiced and carries notes of citrus, but ultimately it is a bitter liqueur. Pairing it with acidity is a recipe for balance—a Tito's take on an apéritif.

> 1½ ounces Tito's Handmade Vodka
> ½ ounce Campari liqueur
> ½ ounce fresh grapefruit juice
> Splash of fresh lime juice
> 1 lime slice, for garnish

Add the Tito's, Campari, grapefruit juice, and lime juice to a shaker with ice. Shake and strain into a glass with a large cube, and garnish with the lime slice.

SUNNY DAZE

Our involvement in philanthropy started in the late '90s with a friend of a friend who needed a favor. An Austin-based organization dedicated to supporting community members living with HIV and AIDS reached out with a small request: Would Tito's be willing to donate a few cases of product to its fundraiser?

We'd do one better; we'd donate the vodka and serve it too. This event became a road map to how Tito's, and every single employee, could make the world a little better—through a simple act of generosity.

It also led to our ongoing mission to give back, which eventually inspired our store. When you shop at the *Love, Tito's* online merch or retail store, all net proceeds from the items we sell—a hat, a dog collar, a hoodie, or a bar tool—go to the nonprofits we work with.

It's like summer in a glass: citrus, berries, and herbs, all harmoniously muddled together and mixed with lemonade to feel like a cool breeze on a hot day. It's earthy, tart, peppery, simply sweet, and most of all, refreshing.

7 blackberries

5 fresh basil leaves

1½ ounces Tito's Handmade Vodka

4 ounces lemonade

½ ounce simple syrup (page 159), optional

Muddle 4 blackberries and 4 basil leaves in a shaker. Add ice, the Tito's, lemonade, and simple syrup and shake. Strain into a glass with ice. Garnish with 3 blackberries on a pick and the remaining basil leaf.

We've only ever asked for one thing in return: If you like our product, tell twenty of your closest friends.
—TITOISM #2

TRUNK PUNCH

Sharing Tito's is part of our DNA. Nonprofits are always on the list, but we don't stop there.

There's no official rule, no meeting to make it happen, it's just known: If you work for Tito's and have a car, you most likely keep a case in your trunk. There's a bottle for every occasion, every person who's never tried it, every cocktail enthusiast who swears they don't like vodka . . . or pledges they'll only drink Tito's. It's a nice gesture for a new friend, the party-saver for spontaneous at-home happy hours, the special thank-you to your barber or your mechanic. And most are given with a quick story and one small request: If you like it, well, you know the drill (see page 123).

Start with three classic Tito's plus ones: cranberry, lemonade, ginger ale. They're all sweet in different ways. A bitter tart, a hint of acidity, and a slight spice. Like jungle juice, it's meant to be shared. We're just . . . elevating it.

> 4 cups Tito's Handmade Vodka
> 8 cups cranberry juice
> 4 cups lemonade
> 4 cups ginger ale
> 5 orange slices

Mix everything up in your favorite punch bowl. Serve over ice and share with a few good friends. Serves 15 to 20.

TITO'S TIP: *Wait to add the ginger ale until your guests arrive to keep the bubbles from going flat.*

VODKA FOR DOG PEOPLE

At Tito's, dogs have always been a part of our story, from the one who was there in the beginning to the strays who found us, and the companions who have worked by our sides ever since. Helping pets and their families has become a pillar of who we are.

We are Vodka for Dog People.

Through the Vodka for Dog People program, we sponsor adoption events and team up with nonprofits that provide spay and neuter services, low-cost vet care, and transport assistance.

Like most folks who are greeted each morning by a paw or a purr, our pets motivate us to be the best versions of ourselves. And they're the reason our conference rooms stay stocked with treats.

Dogs are welcome in nearly every Austin bar, so being *the* dog company just makes sense.

Cardi & Roy, 2019

THE CO-WOOFER

It all started with an ad in the newspaper: *Puppies Available.*

When DogJo was adopted into the Tito's family, we had no idea she'd leave a legacy. From day one, she napped alongside the folks at the Shack and rode shotgun as cases were sampled around town, setting a precedent for the dog-friendly culture here at Tito's.

Tito's co-woofers, 2012

That culture went on to inspire dog-friendly offices across the country and led to a template we've shared with like-minded organizations to encourage workspaces that welcome four-legged friends.

Because your dog isn't just a dog; they're a part of the family. DogJo wasn't just someone's dog, she was a part of the team—the original co-woofer.

Tito's and Grapefruit is already a well-loved drink. Rosemary adds an aromatic layer to the grapefruit's sweet, tart, and bitter notes.

1½ ounces Tito's Handmade Vodka
4 ounces fresh grapefruit juice
1 rosemary sprig, for garnish

Just add Tito's and fresh grapefruit juice to a glass with ice. Stir and garnish with the rosemary sprig.

TITO'S TIP: *Turn your Co-Woofer into a Salty Dog and salt the rim (page 5) before you pour.*

BERRY MUT-TITO

It wasn't long after we broke ground at the distillery that stray dogs started showing up, looking for food, shelter, and a little bit of love. We wanted to help them, so we teamed up with a local nonprofit that was founded right around the time we were, an organization offering low-cost vet care to the pets that needed it most. Once they were healthy, we would find a loving home for each one of them.

Shiner, 2022

All of those strays became a part of our story. We call them distillery dogs.

The distillery dog movement, and the Vodka for Dog People program as a whole, was greatly inspired by a special pup named Stella. She was one of the first strays to cross our path—pregnant, feral, and in bad shape. Without a second thought, our team got her the veterinary care she needed and nursed her back to health, and

Oz, 2019

Stella & Pearl, 2014

Tita, 2014

Taki, 2017

Harper, 2019

when her puppies were born, each one went to a Tito's employee. Stella was the first official "distillery dog" and would become the face of the Vodka for Dog People program.

Stella went from wandering dirt roads alone to traveling the country with the team, shedding light (and a little dog hair) on our animal-related initiatives. Until her final days, in her seventeenth year, she helped us pave the way for dog rescue and proved how full the life of a once-stray distillery dog could be. Without her, the Vodka for Dog People program wouldn't be where it is today.

Over the years, the program's impact continues to grow and the dogs have kept coming. There's Taki, Buddy, Willie, Felix, Oz, Shiner, and over a hundred more.

Let's raise a Berry Mut-Tito in honor of their stories and the many stories to come.

(*recipe continues*)

Willie, 2018

Herbs and berries grow in similar seasons and landscapes, so naturally they work well together. Mint dresses up the berries, adding a cooling sensation to each sip for the ultimate refresher.

1½ ounces Tito's Handmade Vodka
½ ounce simple syrup (page 159)
½ ounce fresh lime juice
6 mint sprigs
4 or 5 fresh blackberries
4 or 5 fresh blueberries
1½ ounces sparkling water

Muddle the Tito's, simple syrup, lime juice, 5 mint sprigs, 2 or 3 blackberries, and 2 or 3 blueberries in a shaker. Add ice and shake, then strain the muddled mixture into a glass with fresh ice and top with sparkling water. Garnish with the remaining berries and mint sprig.

THE CHEW TOY

If it were up to us, dogs would accompany their people on most outings: work, dates, errands, jury duty, happy hours.

While we don't make the rules on most of the above, we know a thing or two about that last one. And we can assure you, they're better with dogs.

Since the creation of the Vodka for Dog People program, Tito's has been part of dog-friendly happy hours all over the country. Sometimes we're raising money for local shelters, other times we're helping adoptable pups find their forever homes, and then there are just those days when we want to meet your dog and give them a bandana. They're the best kind of happy hours.

Pack a water bowl, throw a chew toy in your bag, grab the leash, and you're ready to hit a sunny "paw"tio with your best furriend . . . which is really a treat for everyone.

This is elevated nostalgia in a glass. Swapping grenadine for fresh cherries still creates that classic color but gives the cocktail a tart burst. The Twizzler is just a Twizzler, but it's also a straw, which we think is pretty neat.

5 fresh cherries, pitted
1½ ounces Tito's Handmade Vodka
½ ounce fresh lime juice
4 ounces lemon-lime soda
1 Twizzler, to use as a straw
1 lime slice, for garnish

Muddle 4 of the cherries in a shaker. Add the Tito's, lime juice, and ice. Shake and strain into a glass and top with more ice and the lemon-lime soda. Bite both ends off a Twizzler, turning it into a straw, and use it to stir your drink. Garnish with the lime slice and the remaining cherry.

FOURTEEN ACRES FARM

Mockingbird Distillery is on the outskirts of Austin, where food accessibility is tough. As our distillery grew, a seedling of an idea did too: What if we built a farm to grow fresh produce for the people who work at the distillery?

We weren't farmers, but we could hire a few.

Our soil was made of clay, but we could build raised beds.

Greenhouses were pricey, but we could clean up some used shipping containers and make one ourselves.

We could . . . and we did. And then some.

We plant all types of vegetables, sprinkle in some wildflowers, and run a farmer's market that also stocks the distillery cafeteria. Everything cycles back around—a regenerative farm nurtured from compost, recycled materials, and captured rainwater.

We created an oasis of fresh food off the side of a highway.

RAINWATER

We collect rainwater off the barn, greenhouse roofs, and other distillery buildings to keep our farm operation going strong even in our hottest months. It's an environmentally friendly way to nourish our produce.

Plus, there's something about a summer storm. Those vast Texas skies open up, lightning flashes across the landscape, and thunder shakes the ground, leaving behind a purple-hued sunset when the clouds clear.

———— ★ ————

Lavender and lemon: a lovely color palette and a lovelier cocktail. Lavender syrup is sweet and floral and can be an acquired taste. A healthy amount of fresh lemon complements the cocktail's natural herbaceous notes.

> 1½ ounces Tito's Handmade Vodka
> 1 ounce fresh lemon juice
> ½ ounce lavender simple syrup (page 162)
> 2 ounces sparkling water
> 1 food-safe dried lavender sprig, for garnish

Add the Tito's, lemon juice, and lavender syrup to a shaker with ice and shake. Strain into a glass with ice and top with the sparkling water. Garnish with the dried lavender sprig.

GO SEASONAL

On the farm, we're more aware of
the seasons than we are when we're
walking down the aisle of a grocery
store. For the freshest cocktails,
we suggest working with what the
season has to offer.

GREEN DREAM

Toast, guac, masks:
Avocado does it all.
    May as well mix it
with Tito's.
    This drink's got
a hint of springtime, a
dash of your favorite
green smoothie, and
the vibe of a blended
mojito.

———— ★ ————

Sure, avocado may seem like an odd fruit to add to a shaker, but its neutrality acts as a nice foundation for the cocktail's stronger flavors of mint and lime. Plus, its creamy texture is exactly what you want in a blended drink.

> 4 fresh mint leaves, torn
> 1½ ounces Tito's Handmade Vodka
> 2 ounces avocado simple syrup (page 160)
> ½ ounce fresh lime juice
> 1 ounce sparkling water
> 1 fresh mint sprig, for garnish

Muddle the 4 torn mint leaves in a shaker, then add the Tito's and let them combine for a few minutes. Toss in your avocado simple syrup, lime juice, and a handful of ice and shake for at least 30 seconds, letting the mixture water down slightly. Strain everything into a glass with ice and top with the sparkling water and the fresh mint sprig.

LULING SPECIAL

Watermelon seed–spitting competitions are a real thing, at least in Texas.

Some of the first Tito's employees have even participated, venturing to Luling, Texas, where we originally came across a city-wide display of seed-spitting prowess. We have yet to take home the gold, but we'll always settle for a good drink and a good time.

——————— ★ ———————

Watermelon has a trifecta of flavor: sweet, slightly bitter, hints of sour. Raspberry and lime make it tarter, and basil adds savory notes of pepper. The egg white softens the acidity, rounding out each ingredient while punctuating the cocktail with a perfect foam layer.

½ cup basil-watermelon juice (recipe follows)
2 ounces Tito's Handmade Vodka
1 ounce fresh lime juice
1 large egg white
¼ cup raspberries, plus a few more for garnish
Splash of sparkling water
1 fresh basil leaf, for garnish

Add the basil-watermelon juice, Tito's, lime juice, egg white, and ¼ cup raspberries to a shaker with ice. Shake it up for at least 30 seconds, then pour everything into a glass and top with a splash of sparkling water. Garnish with the basil leaf and a few raspberries.

BASIL-WATERMELON JUICE

4 cups fresh, cubed watermelon
¼ cup fresh basil leaves

In a blender, combine the watermelon and basil leaves. Strain and refrigerate in an airtight container for up to 3 days.

SPICED CIDER

Pairs well with apple
picking and leaf peeping
(and takes the edge off
family holidays).
      It's anything but
basic.

———————— ★ ————————

Sugar, spice, and everything spiked. Hot cider topped with Tito's is great on its own. Adding citrus brightens the cocktail, while ginger adds zest to cinnamon's warm bite. A sprinkle of salt intensifies each flavor so you're able to taste all of these elements in every sip.

6 ounces Tito's Handmade Vodka
10 ounces apple cider
2 ounces orange liqueur
¾ ounce fresh lemon juice
4 teaspoons maple simple syrup (page 162)
¼ teaspoon kosher salt
1 teaspoon ginger paste
¼ teaspoon ground cinnamon
1 thin apple slice, for garnish

Combine the Tito's, apple cider, orange liqueur, lemon juice, maple simple syrup, salt, ginger paste, and cinnamon in a saucepan. Stir over medium heat, heating slowly for 5 to 10 minutes until it reaches your desired temperature. We suggest cutting the heat right before it starts boiling. Pour into your favorite mug and garnish with the apple slice. Serves 2 to 4.

CLEMENTINE CHEER

The soft crunch you hear when you step into snow—it's that kind of crisp.

The "candles lit, pie in the oven, fire crackling" feeling when you step back inside—it's that kind of spice.

And sure, you'll have to peel a lot of clementines. But we promise the juice is worth the squeeze with this winter citrus favorite.

———— ★ ————

When the holiday season arrives, it seems like every house is filled with wafts of cinnamon, citrus, and savory herbs. Why not throw 'em into a glass and top it with some holiday cheer (aka booze).

1½ ounces Tito's Handmade Vodka
2 ounces fresh-squeezed clementine juice
½ ounce cinnamon simple syrup (page 160)
2 ounces ginger ale
1 fresh sage leaf, for garnish

Add the Tito's, clementine juice, and cinnamon simple syrup to a shaker with ice. Shake and strain into a glass with fresh ice. Top with the ginger ale and garnish with the sage leaf.

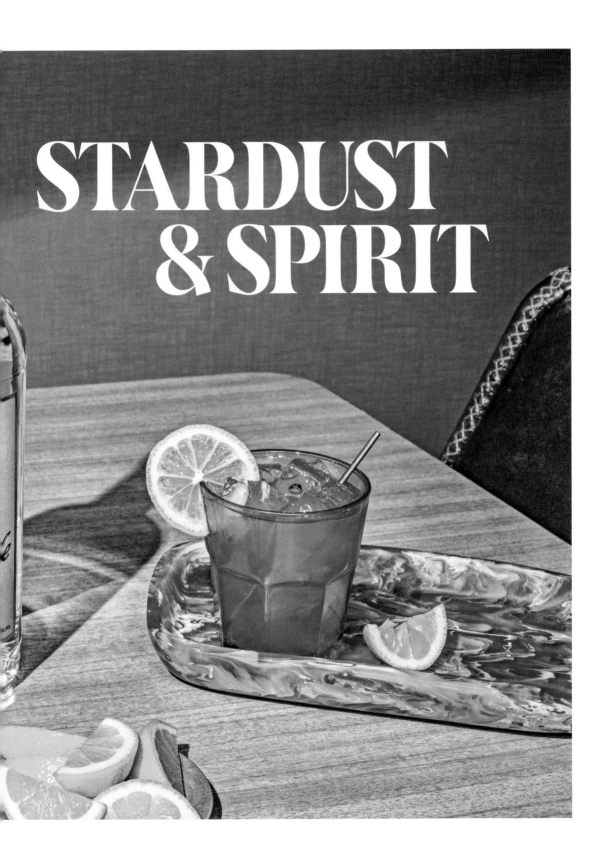

STARDUST & SPIRIT

Here at Tito's, we've always said that we're made of stardust. We know it sounds a little woo-woo, but stick with us for a second. Scientifically speaking, humans are quite literally made of stardust; we share about 97 percent of the same kinds of atoms and elements that make up our galaxy. This appeals to the scientific-minded—that which can be sampled and measured. Yet *stardust,* the word itself, speaks to the poet, the dreamer, and the spirit in each of us. It makes us pause and think about magic and beauty in the world, expansive possibility, adventures into the unknown, and the very tangible but nevertheless enigmatic feeling that we're all cosmically connected. It's that feeling of connection mixed with the pins-and-needles of possibility that drives us to do good, that makes all of us *want* to do good.

And so, with this stardust theme as a guiding force under the surface of pretty much everything at Tito's Handmade Vodka, we try to do just that and connect with all kinds of people and organizations who are out there trying to do good things too. Through the years, we've ended up with our own kind of expansive network of connected constellations. In similar form to the actual cosmos, the one through which we're hurtling right now, there are new frontiers every time we're able to glimpse past the horizon we always thought was as far as we could go—unexplored galaxies, planetary possibilities, and even new constellations to draw between stars we've known about since the beginning. We like it this way. There's never an ending. But there's always a reason to pause, pour a drink, and say thank you. To raise that glass to everyone who's played a starring role in this copper cosmos. Because Tito's just wouldn't be Tito's without every single one of 'em.

We could list names for pages and pages, so instead, we'll take a macro approach and address the constellations instead of each and every star.

Fans and believers, old and new, and everyone since who's tried Tito's, loved it, told their friends, and kept on believing in that copper-capped bottle.

Bartenders pouring drinks and advocating for us from behind bars everywhere, and mixologists creating new spins and experiences with our vodka.

Account owners and buyers stocking their shelves and backbars, featuring Tito's on menus, placing our bottles front and center, and becoming fellow friends in a hard-and-fast industry.

Distributors who work tirelessly to get cases and bottles into stores and bars, especially those who gave us a chance way back when, before anyone knew who we were.

Nonprofits and organizations that inspire us with their passion and spirit and invite us to join their communities and share their causes.

Creative collaborators who have understood our goals and visions and, from them, made impactful, beautiful designs, images, and stories to share with the world.

Team Tito's, the individuals who bring the Tito's spirit to life and keep us moving forward. They embody our passion for giving back, believe in our story and make it their own, and are always ready to share a bottle and raise a glass.

And dogs, always the dogs.

Thank you.

Thank you for believing in our dream, and for inspiring us to do good.

Here's to you.

STARDUST SIPPER

Orange and lemon are an obvious pair; citrus loves citrus. Throw in some spice from cinnamon and cool sweetness from vanilla and the citrus's acidity is slightly neutralized, keeping your cocktail light and smooth.

> Cinnamon, to rim your glass
> Lemon zest, to rim your glass
> Sugar, to rim your glass
> 1½ ounces Tito's Handmade Vodka
> 1 ounce fresh lemon juice
> ¾ ounce orange liqueur
> ¾ ounce cinnamon-vanilla simple syrup
> (page 160)
> 1 lemon twist, for garnish

Combine equal parts cinnamon, lemon zest, and sugar and rim your glass (page 5). Add the Tito's, lemon juice, orange liqueur, and cinnamon-vanilla simple syrup to a shaker with ice. Shake and strain into your glass. Garnish with the lemon twist.

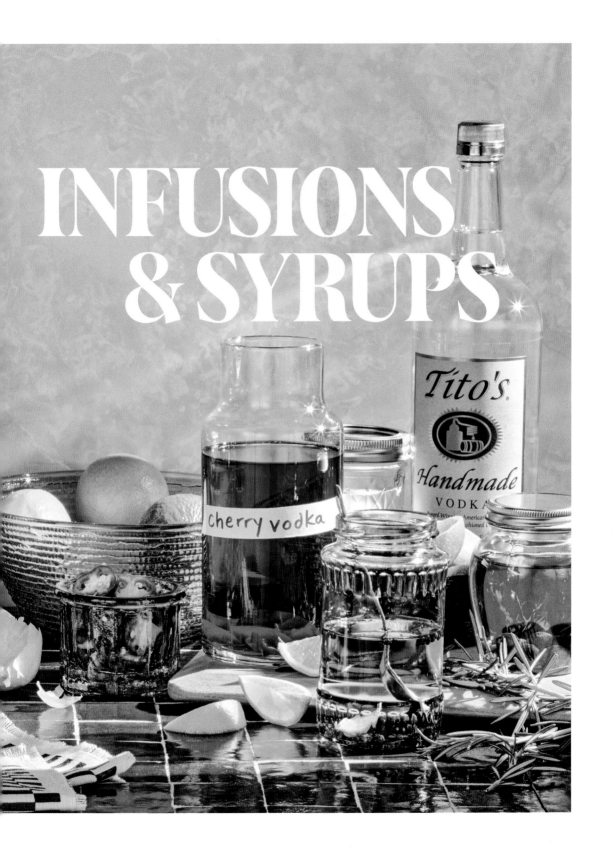

INFUSIONS & SYRUPS

INFUSIONS

Infusions are a simple science. Each ingredient reacts differently when it sits in a jar full of vodka. That's why it's fun. A little bit of this, a little more of that, a sprinkle of something else—variation is always at your fingertips.

Start with an equation:

TITO'S + INGREDIENT + TIME = A REALLY GOOD INFUSION

Combine Tito's and whatever produce, spice, or herb you're in the mood for in a jar with a lid, give it a shake, and taste every now and then. Once your desired flavor is reached, remove the ingredients; use a cheesecloth, strainer, colander, or anything comparable. See, it's simple, but it's also science.

Plus, we've got some tips and tricks to make any infusion that much more delicious.

- FRUIT AND BERRIES: Flash-freeze the fruit for 1 to 3 hours, depending on how much time you've got, before infusing. As fruit freezes, the water in the fruit expands, breaking down its cell walls; when it thaws, all the color and flavor is extracted and brought to the surface.
- HOT PEPPERS: Spice is a spectrum, but peppers infuse fast. For middle-of-the-road heat, let 'em sit for 30 to 60 minutes. If you want a little less fire, remove the cluster of seeds attached to the pith, along with the pith itself. The pith actually has most of the capsaicin (aka the chemical compound that brings the heat), not necessarily the seeds. That being said, seeds don't offer the best texture, so feel free to remove those too.
- PEELS, SEEDS, AND PITH: Best practice is to lose the peel, remove the seeds if you can, and take off the pith (the white, stringy pieces left behind on a fruit or the white rib inside a pepper).

- **COLD, DARK, OR BOTH:** Most infusions can go without refrigeration, just make sure to keep them covered and stored in a cool, dark place while they're doing their thing. If you're following our recipes, we'll specify which ones need to be in the fridge.

All the recipes below call for 750 mL of Tito's Handmade Vodka. Depending on the size of your container, it may be a little less. But that's the beauty of infusion-making: It's all an experiment. Use whatever resealable jar you've got— pickle, pasta sauce, olive, jam. Adjust quantities based on what you're using and go with your gut. Figure out what works, what you like, and have fun doing it.

We just laid the groundwork:

Infusion	Ingredient	Infuse For . . .	Goes Great In . . .	Good For . . .
APPLE & CINNAMON	2 apples, sliced and seeded 2 cinnamon sticks	5 days	hot or cold cider	2 weeks in cool, dark place
BLUEBERRY	1 pint blueberries	5 to 7 days	lemonade	2 weeks in cool, dark place
CUCUMBER	1 cucumber, peeled and sliced	1 to 2 days	sparkling water with lemon	5 days in cool, dark place
GARLIC & BLACK PEPPER	½ cup black peppercorns and 2 garlic cloves	1 to 2 days	Bloody Marys	1 month in cool, dark place
GREEN TEA	1 or 2 green tea bags or 2 to 3 teaspoons loose-leaf tea	8 to 24 hours, shaking every so often	still water with honey and lemon	2 weeks in cool, dark place
JALAPEÑO	1 jalapeño, sliced and seeded	30 to 60 minutes	TitoRitas or Bloody Marys	1 month in freezer
LEMON	3 lemons, sliced and seeded	3 to 4 days	lemonade or sparkling water	2 weeks in cool, dark place
ORANGE	2 oranges, sliced and seeded	4 days	Screwdrivers or sparkling water	2 weeks in cool, dark place
PEACH	2 peaches, sliced and pitted	4 to 6 days	Mules or lemonade	2 weeks in cool, dark place
PEAR	5 pears, sliced and seeded	4 to 5 days	Mules or sparkling water with lemon	2 weeks in cool, dark place
PEPPERMINT CANDIES	10 peppermint candies or 2 to 3 candy canes, crushed	1 to 2 days or until candies dissolve	hot chocolate	1 month in cool, dark place
PINEAPPLE	6 pineapple rings	5 to 7 days	coconut water	2 weeks in refrigerator
ROSE	½ cup edible rose petals	3 to 5 days, shaking daily	sparkling water with lemon and grenadine	1 week in cool, dark place
ROSEMARY	4 to 5 fresh rosemary sprigs	6 to 8 hours	Mules or lemonade	1 week in cool, dark place
VANILLA	2 whole vanilla beans, split down the middle	5 to 7 days, shaking daily	hot chocolate	1 month in cool, dark place
WATERMELON	1 small watermelon, cubed	4 to 5 days	Mules or sparkling water	1 week in refrigerator

SYRUPS

Just like flavored vodka, you always have the option of buying flavored syrups off the shelf. But where's the fun in that?

Take a page from our infusions and try making flavored syrups yourself. That way, you know exactly what's in them and how they'll taste. Plus, it's a chance to impress your friends. "Oh, this cinnamon-vanilla simple syrup? No big deal. I made it myself and put it in this ornate, reusable jar."

Not to mention, DIYing your favorite cocktail syrups also comes with an easy-to-remember equation:

SUGAR (OR OTHER SWEETENER) + INGREDIENT + WATER = A REALLY GOOD FLAVORED SYRUP

See what we mean? *Simple* is in the name for a reason.

Each recipe yields about 1¼ cups.

SIMPLE SYRUP

1 cup sugar
1 cup water

Combine the sugar and water in a saucepan over medium heat and stir until all the sugar dissolves. Let cool and then refrigerate in an airtight container for up to 1 month.

AVOCADO SIMPLE SYRUP

1 cup sugar
1 cup water
1 avocado, peeled and pitted

Combine the sugar and water in a saucepan over medium heat and stir until all the sugar dissolves. Let cool, then transfer the mixture to a blender, add the avocado, and purée until smooth. Refrigerate in an airtight container for up to 5 days.

SIMPLE COCKTAIL SUGGESTION: *Tito's Spiked Smoothie*

CINNAMON-VANILLA SIMPLE SYRUP

1 cup sugar
1 cup water
6 cinnamon sticks
1 teaspoon vanilla extract*

Combine the sugar and water in a saucepan over medium heat and stir until all the sugar dissolves. Remove from heat and add the cinnamon sticks and vanilla, then cover and let steep for 1 hour. After an hour, remove the cinnamon sticks. Refrigerate in an airtight container for up to 1 month.

Want plain cinnamon simple syrup? Just omit the vanilla.

SIMPLE COCKTAIL SUGGESTIONS: *Tito's Hot Chocolate, Tito's Hot Toddy*

GINGER-HONEY SIMPLE SYRUP

1 cup honey
1 cup water
¾ cup fresh ginger, peeled and sliced

Combine all the ingredients in a saucepan and bring to a boil. Reduce the heat and gently simmer, uncovered, for about 15 to 30 minutes, stirring occasionally. Remove from heat, strain, and let cool before using. Refrigerate in an airtight container for up to 1 month.

SIMPLE COCKTAIL SUGGESTION: *Tito's Mule*

HIBISCUS-GINGER SIMPLE SYRUP

1 cup sugar
1 cup water
½ cup food-safe dried hibiscus flowers
1 tablespoon fresh ginger, peeled and sliced

Combine all the ingredients in a saucepan and bring to a boil. Reduce the heat and gently simmer, uncovered, for about 15 to 30 minutes, stirring occasionally. Remove from heat, let cool, and then refrigerate for 2 hours. Strain before using. Refrigerate in an airtight container for up to 2 weeks.

SIMPLE COCKTAIL SUGGESTIONS: *Tito's & Lemonade, Tito's Sour, Tito's Gimlet*

HONEY SIMPLE SYRUP

1 cup honey
1 cup water

Combine all the ingredients in a saucepan over medium heat and stir until the honey is dissolved. Let cool before using. Refrigerate in an airtight container for up to 1 month.

(Why not just add honey directly to your drink? For a chilled cocktail, honey is too thick to dissolve properly, leaving a glob at the bottom of your glass.)

SIMPLE COCKTAIL SUGGESTIONS: *Tito's & Lemonade, Tito's Mule*

LAVENDER SIMPLE SYRUP

1 cup sugar
1 cup water
3 tablespoons food-safe dried lavender

Combine all the ingredients in a saucepan over medium heat and stir until the sugar is dissolved. Strain and let cool before using. Refrigerate in an airtight container for up to 2 weeks.

SIMPLE COCKTAIL SUGGESTIONS: *Tito's & Lemonade, Tito's Sour*

MAPLE SIMPLE SYRUP

1 cup maple syrup
1 cup water

Combine all the ingredients in a saucepan over medium heat and stir until the maple syrup is dissolved. Let cool before using. Refrigerate in an airtight container for up to 1 month.

SIMPLE COCKTAIL SUGGESTIONS: *Tito's Hot Chocolate, Tito's Hot Toddy*

PECAN SIMPLE SYRUP

1 cup halved pecans
1 cup sugar
1 cup water

Combine all ingredients in a saucepan over medium heat. Bring to a simmer and stir until the sugar dissolves. Continue to stir and let simmer for about 5 minutes. Strain and let cool before using. Refrigerate in an airtight container for up to 2 weeks.

SIMPLE COCKTAIL SUGGESTIONS: *Tito's Hot Chocolate, Tito's Hot Toddy, Tito's Espresso Martini*

ACKNOWLEDGMENTS

WORDS

Daniela Young

Josie Fox

DRINKS

Spatchcock Funk

Alex DeRosa

Matt Read

Independent Contributors

Christina Rhodes

Abdul J. Ford

Tony Abou-Ganim

PHOTOGRAPHY

Piacere, Creative Production Agency
(ii-iii, xiii, 6–7, 10, 13, 14, 18, 22, 25,
28–29, 33, 34, 38–39, 40, 44–45,
50, 53, 54, 57, 68, 71, 76, 78, 81,
88, 91, 92, 95, 101, 102, 105, 109,
110, 112, 114, 120, 128, 133, 134,
139, 140, 143, 144, 147, 164, 168)

Adam Cantiello, producer

Michael James Murray, photographer
& director

Michael Persico, photographer

Emilie Fosnocht, prop stylist

Kelsi Windmiller, prop & set stylist

Kit Ramsey and Georgia Wescott,
styling assistants

Ej Bernard, photo assistant

Neal Santos, photo assistant

Ed Newton, DIT

Michael Moschella and Arturo Zarate,
production assistants

Taylor Saya Shaw, retoucher

Cody Cooper, studio manager

Courtney Kehr, studio assistant

Beyond Creative Management
(cover, xiv-1, 17, 30, 123, 148–149,
154–155, 157, 178)

Johnny Autry, photography

Charlotte Autry, styling

Independent Contributors

Josie Fox (i, iv–v, vi–vii, viii, 8, 15, 26, 47, 56, 58, 60, 63, 64, 74–75, 79, 82, 87, 98–99, 106, 116–117, 119, 131, 153, 168, 176)

Dylan Makar (98–99, 136–137)

Taylor Morgan (96–97)

Tonya Schabacker (12, 21, 66, 124, 130–131)

Tito's Archival Images (42, 43, 126, 129, 130)

COVER DESIGN

Alicia Nguyen

LITERARY AGENT

The Gernert Company

Anna Worrall

HARPERCOLLINS TEAM

Stephanie Fletcher and Jacqueline Quirk, editorial

Renata De Oliveira, interior design

Jennifer Eck, managing editorial

Hope Breeman, production editorial

Katie Tull and Beatrice Jason, marketing

Anwesha Basu and Sarah Falter, publicity

This idea started with a stack of cocktail books borrowed from the Austin Public Library. In the time it took to publish *Spirit in a Bottle*, we learned invaluable insights, some inspired by those books, some from our own journey to write and publish this one. Most importantly, however, we learned that there was still a lot to learn about Tito's.

Cocktail exploration was a given. How does violet liqueur compare to lavender? What happens when you serve the Nightcap chilled, instead of room temp? Is a martini with no vermouth really just a glass of ice-cold Tito's? But those questions came a little later.

The foundation of this book was built on the conversations we had with our team and friends of the brand. The folks who have Tito's stories from way back when, who are mixology experts and barware connoisseurs, the ones who helped craft the voice you read on every page of this book, and the ones who are always willing to taste-test a cocktail . . . for the sake of research.

Special thanks to this incredible group for getting us here: Allie, Beth, Brian Floyd, Bryan, Caitlin, Elizabeth, Kevin, Lisa, Pete, Ryan, Taylor, Zach Golden.

INDEX

NOTE: Page references in *italics* refer to photos of recipes.

ABOUT
TITO'S HANDMADE VODKA

Dreamed up and distilled in Austin, Texas, Tito's Handmade Vodka was founded by sixth-generation Texan Tito Beveridge. Since selling our first case back in 1997, Tito's has gained a reputation for our high-quality product, charitable contributions, and goal to make people happy while making the world a better place. Inspired by the distillation methods of fine single-malt scotches and high-end French Cognacs, our vodka is made in old-fashioned pot stills, designed to be savored in an ice-cold martini or a simple Tito's Soda Lime. Crafted in batches with each batch taste-tested, Tito's goes down smooth and has an impeccably clean finish.

HarperCollins books may be purchased for educational, business, or sales promotional use. For information, please email the Special Markets Department at SPsales@harpercollins.com.

FIRST EDITION

DESIGNED BY RENATA DE OLIVEIRA

Photography credits start on page 165.

Library of Congress Cataloging-in-Publication Data has been applied for.

ISBN 978-0-06-328210-0

24 25 26 27 28   TC   10 9 8 7 6 5 4 3 2 1